The Year of My Life

reminiscences and rants

Politics

by Mark I. Jacobson

I0423944

Coming to Amazon.com and BN.com in 2017:

The Year of My Life: reminiscences and rants 2016

Reflections on the good, the bad, and boy did it get ugly!

The Year of My Life: reminiscences and rants Violence

From online bullying to ongoing war, why non-violence is a non-issue.

Copyright © 2016 by Mark I. Jacobson
All rights reserved. This book or any portion
thereof may not be reproduced or used in
any manner whatsoever without the express
written permission of the publisher except for
the use of brief quotations in a book review.
Printed in the United States of America
First Printing, 2016
ISBN 1-5350701-1-0
The Year of My Life
P.O. Box 80686
Las Vegas, NV 89180
www.TheYearOfMyLife.com

This collection of reminiscences and rants is dedicated to my folks Herbert and Essie. It is also dedicated to Victoria Juliet Schoonover and Lesley Ellen Marchese. Before they left, they made sure I knew that I was loved. Without that, this book would not have been possible.

TABLE OF CONTENTS

PROLOGUE

It all started in 1953. It was a cold October day. It should have been a cold January day because that was the actual target month for my birth, but things don't always work according to plan. That's a lesson I've learned, literally, from birth. To be honest, that was probably the last time that I was early for anything. My birth certificate states that I showed up at precisely 9:00 AM, on the 15th of October. I weighed 2 pounds 11 ounces and my parents later told me that I could fit in a shoebox. Ironically, shoes would be the least of my concerns for the next several years.

Now you may think that you're about to read a feel good story about overcoming obstacles. You are not. I did overcome obstacles, to an extent, but this isn't really a book about me. I just thought that the best way to introduce myself was to start at the beginning and that's about as beginning as you're ever going to get. If you're really interested in what happened next, I will be weaving my personal life into this story whenever the need arises. But this is really a story about you or more precisely, us. It's a book about how you and I exist and interact with each other. You could call this book a literary selfie because it is about world and national events which have and continue to shape our lives. It is also about my personal feelings and beliefs about these events. As I said, along the way I will intersperse my vision of life as I overcame obstacles both internally and externally. By the end of this book all those insights should create a nice portrait of us.

As with most rants, it's really difficult to stop at just one. If I were to put all my rants into one book, it would make Tolstoy's "War and Peace" look like a short story. I also have more than enough reminiscences, some short and some much longer, that coincide with my rants. So I've decided to break one book up into several books, each with its own topic. I can't say how many books that will end up being because each day brings another rant. I can only hope that you will continue to laugh, cry, and get angry along with me.

There is a reason why this book is titled "The Year of My Life: reminiscences and rants." I'll give you a clue, it has very little to do with any one year of my life. As a writer, I have two things in common with all writers. First, I have a lot of opinions. Now that may not seem unusual because every human being on this planet has an opinion about something. But when you become a feature writer, you become an observer of life. You also learn that every observation and opinion should be backed up by the facts. The second thing that I have in common with all other writers, is that I love to write. If I ever lose that love I will cease being a writer or, in the worst case scenario, cease breathing.

So that's what this book is all about. Now let me tell you what this book is not about. This book is not about me being the last word on everything. Even though my opinions will be backed up by logic or facts, they are still my opinions. I encourage you to engage in intelligent debate whenever possible. Let me repeat that, I encourage you engage in intelligent debate with me. That means debate based on logic or facts. It doesn't mean name calling or backing up your opinion with unsubstantiated rhetoric written by someone else with an opinion or an agenda. If you don't come back at me with logic or facts, I won't come back to you at all.

So how can you reach me? You can go to TheYearOfMyLife.com and leave me a message. You can send me an email: Opinion@TheYearOfMyLife.com. You can also go to my Facebook page: facebook.com/TheYearOfMyLife or Twitter feed: @TheYearOfMyLife and join the conversation. From time to time, I'll be hosting a live give and take on my Google Hangouts page or a live stream on my YouTube page. The dates and times will be posted on my Facebook page and Twitter feeds.

I probably should tell you that you're not going to like everything I have to say. Some of my reminiscences may make you feel good about yourself, your community, your country, and your world. But some of my rants may have the opposite effect and leave you feeling angry. That's good because, in life, it's impossible to have one without the other. I will try to make the transition from one to the other as painless as possible.

My ultimate objective with this book is to foster some sort of alternative discussion on topics that are discussed often or, in some cases, not often enough. I will try to introduce a different perspective with the former and enlighten with the latter. Although this is a book about my reminiscences and rants, I will always endeavor to show both sides of the story. One thing I've learned as a reporter and writer is that there is always at least one more side to the story.

So why am I writing a book about politics? The answer is simple. With everything that has happened during the presidential campaign of 2016, this book practically wrote itself. But my interest in the political system began many years ago on a political planet far, far away (yes, I am blatantly pandering to Star Wars fans) while I was still a politically naïve high school student.

Like most high schools, we held elections for the student council. To be honest, the student council really couldn't accomplish anything of any consequence. It was forced to operate under the oversight and control of the board of education, the principal of Lawrence high school, and anyone else in a position of authority. But it was a "democracy" of sorts in that the members were elected to their positions by their fellow students. And that in itself was an interesting phenomenon because most of the students didn't care about issues as much as they cared about the excitement of being a part of political theater. Sound familiar? It should because that has been at the very core of every U.S. election since I first cast a vote, in 1972, and probably much longer.

Now I don't mean to dismiss elections as nothing more than the culmination of fun and games. In many parts of the world, elections are anything but that. An ink stained finger is the symbol of hope and, in some cases, defiance of the threat of death in the pursuit of that hope. But in recent years the political process in this country has become nothing more than a contest between personalities and their minions. Today, elections are not so much about contesting issues and the welfare of the country as they are about determining the outcomes of popularity contests. Even though voters have created this game show system of politics, they are quick to blame politicians when that same system comes to a complete halt. There's enough blame to go around.

Finally, I would like to say that the purpose of the stories within this book series is to entertain as well as inform. Portions of these books were written with my tongue planted firmly in my cheek because humor has always been a very important part of my life. It has been my constant companion through some very good times and, especially, some very bad times. You'll find a fair amount of sarcasm and innuendo in these pages. I will try to keep most of that within parentheses; but there are times when a little may sneak out without notice. There will also be times when these books will take a serious turn. There should be no question in your mind as to when those moments occur. I have tried to strike a balance between serious and humorous moments; but if there is ever any question in your mind, humor will always win out.

I've had a love/hate relationship with this book since the first day that I stared at a blank computer screen and wondered what I had gotten myself into. There were times when I absolutely hated writing it. There were other times when I loved watching this book come together. So if you love this book, I agree. If you hate this book, I agree (yes, I am blatantly pandering to every reader). And with those words, I think I feel a rant coming on.

CHAPTER 1 - PULLING THE PLUG

As I said, I first voted for president of the United States in 1972. I was a registered Democrat because, quite frankly, my parents were Democrats. You usually pull the same political lever as your parents when you vote in your inaugural presidential election. I was no exception. Most of my friends were Democrats and the community that I grew up in was largely comprised of Democrats. There was one glaring exception. The father of one of my best friends was a Republican. To be honest, his was not the only Republican family in my hometown of Cedarhurst. But I bring this up for a very important reason. Dave's family was a shining example of one of the main points that I am trying to make with this book.

As far back as I can remember, Andrew J. Parise lived a political life. First off, he was chief of staff for seven town supervisors in the nearby town of Hempstead. He also served on our local village board and as deputy mayor. He ended his political career as mayor of Cedarhurst for two decades.

Dave's dad was a politician. More importantly, he was a lifelong Republican and patriarch of a Republican family. My dad was a lifelong Democrat and patriarch of a family of Democrats. I could tell you dozens of awkward moment stories that would happen whenever our two families got together. You know what I'm talking about; the small differences of opinion that somehow escalate into debates, name calling, and the occasional insult. I could tell you those stories but I would have to make them up because there were none. Dave's family and my family were fast friends.

You see, when I was growing up having a differing political belief didn't make you a bad person. We looked at each other as intelligent individuals who just happened to have a difference of opinion when it came to politics. Come to think of it, that's the exact same way in which we dealt with religion. Although my community was predominantly Jewish, not all my friends were Jewish. Dave was one of my non-Jewish friends but his family would assist with Jewish causes. My family would assist with non-Jewish causes because we saw them only as causes without a secular name tag. But that's for another book.

And so, our families were the antithesis of the political polarization that has become popular in the American political system. Our families exemplified how not to allow political office seekers to create divisiveness within the vast community of voters who, ultimately, put them into office. These days, it seems as if the electorate is locked into a perpetual game of good guys versus bad guys. It's a child's game played by adults. Politicians and their political parties make up the rules as they go along.

When I was old enough, I registered as a Democrat. I was an idealistic eighteen-year-old who believed that the party's platform mirrored my own values. Sounds good doesn't it? If only that was the truth, the whole truth, and nothing but the truth. Actually, there was another, more important reason why I became a registered Democrat... I was greedy.

Cedarhurst is a relatively sleepy little community on the western end of Long Island, New York. Long Island is divided into two counties. Suffolk County, the wealthier and larger portion of the island, stretches outward into the Atlantic Ocean. It's only connection to land is by way of Nassau County to the west. Not to be outdone by its brother to the east; Nassau County has its own little caste system, namely the north shore and the south shore. The north shore, where the likes of F. Scott and Zelda Fitzgerald would party until dawn's early light, is considered upper class. The south shore, of which Cedarhurst plays a small part, is more working class.

The name Nassau harkens back to the early days of colonialism when the Dutch established a settlement. Even the county seal, a raging lion, is strangely similar to the seal in the province of Limburg in the Netherlands. Cedarhurst is one part of a geographic area collectively known as

"The Five Towns." The other four towns aren't really that important unless, of course, you live there. It's situated four miles from the former Idlewild airport, now JFK. The airport was renamed less than a month after the assassination of President Kennedy and roughly two months past my tenth birthday.

President Kennedy's assassination happened on a Friday. I spent the weekend thinking that a sniper could be hiding anywhere and watching me. I wasn't alone in feeling terrorized. Today, we classify terrorism by the number of people killed or injured. Back then the number was one. The country was terrorized and would remain that way throughout the sixties. But I digress. We'll come back to this later.

Cedarhurst is also located about 14 miles from New York City. The end of the Second World War and the introduction of the GI bill gave soldiers the opportunity for homeownership. My father, a young second lieutenant, took advantage of that opportunity and settled down in this 'wooded area of cedars,' a throwback to our national and familial UK roots. Its proximity to the country's most populous city was enough to give it a relatively new designation, the suburbs.

One of the most interesting things about growing up in Cedarhurst was understanding how politically plugged in it was to the larger county of Nassau or as I called it, the mother ship. Then, as now, political parties in power had the ability to manipulate the status quo in favor of the status quid pro quo. In the late sixties to early seventies, just as I was entering my late teens, the state and local Democratic political stars aligned. The timing was perfect because although I was idealistic, I could have easily sold out my idealism for the promise of a summer job. Fortunately for me, I never had to go over to the dark side (yes, once again, I am blatantly pandering to Star Wars fans). Hey, I told you I was greedy.

Anyway, that's pretty much the way things worked in those days. If you were a member of the party in power, you knew somebody who knew somebody who knew somebody. All of a sudden things happened. It was kind of like the Mafia without all the great Italian food. It still works that way today. Political party fervor gets you political party favors. And so it goes.

Being plugged into a local political party gives you access to local politics. That may not seem like anything much but whether you are running for city council or president of the United States, all politics is local. That means that the only thing that matters to voters is how anything at any level of government affects them. So if you're a local politician and a constituent's handicapped son needs a summer job, you do your best to find him a summer job. Keep in mind that this was way before the Americans with Disabilities Act. It would be another twenty years before disabled job seekers would receive equal protection under the law (I would say that this is blatant pandering to disabled people but since I am one, I don't think it counts).

That was the beginning of my life as a Democrat. I started out a lot more liberal but at this point in my life, I've moved more towards the center. That happens with age and knowledge. Who am I kidding? It has nothing to do with either one of those. It has everything to do with a more finely tuned bullshit meter that allows me to tell when someone is blowing smoke up my ass or talking out of theirs.

You don't need to be a certain age or at a certain educational level to know when you're being played by politicians. All you have to realize is that getting the job comes first, keeping the job comes second, and everything else comes third. But politicians keep the smoke screen up with silly little catch phrases, cheering crowds, and loud rock music. That only serves to numb voters into believing that they've hitched their wagons to a workhorse who is only interested in getting the job done.

But that job doesn't get done by any one individual or any one party. It was designed as a collaborative effort for a very good reason. You see contrary to popular belief; our Founding Fathers were not the visionaries or paragons of virtue that they've been made out to be. They were human beings with human flaws. Realizing this, checks and balances were built into our governmental system in order to keep individual power and ambition from running amok. Let me give you one example that specifically relates to two of our Founding Fathers.

When I mention the Boston tea party, what's the first thing that comes to mind? I'd be willing to bet that it's taxation without representation. The implication is that England had been unfairly taxing the colonies for quite some time. Finally, the colonists revolted when an unfair tax was levied upon the importation of tea. Dressed up like Indians, they boarded the cargo ships and dumped all the tea into Boston Harbor. That's what I learned and believed until I started to research this book. It turns out that there's a lot more to this story.

John "sign on the dotted line" Hancock and Samuel "toss down a cold one (for visitors from the other side of the pond, warm one)" Adams, wore many hats. Sam Adams was sometimes a brewer and at other times a newspaper publisher. John Hancock inherited a shipping business, the House of Hancock. They would both go on to become Founding Fathers of a country and governors of one of the states in that country. They were also smugglers and tax evaders. Which brings us back to the Boston tea party.

At the time, having colonies on the other side of the ocean seemed like a good idea to the British. That is until the colonists started getting into fights with everyone from the Indians to the Canadians. The cost of supporting and protecting these future independent Americans was bankrupting the Bank of England. King George III attempted to raise money by taxing the colonists in several different ways, most of which affected wealthy businessman. But he soon found out that enforcing the collection of those taxes was not an easy task. It turns out that wealthy businessmen don't like to pay taxes -- go figure.

So the king came up with a plan B. He gave an exclusive trade license to the mega-conglomerate, the East India Trading Company. The license allowed them to sell British tea to America. The cost of the tea would be much less than the colonists were already paying for Dutch tea. The money that he would receive from the East India Trading Company would help to offset the costs that England was incurring in America. Sounds like a win-win for everyone; that is, everyone but Sam and John. These two Founding Fathers were making a pretty penny smuggling Dutch tea into the colonies. They knew that if tea consumers got a better deal, they were out of business. So they devised a plan to get rid of the competition. That was how the Boston tea party came into play and the rest is, well, history.

And so, in the end, it wasn't retaliation over political and economic oppression that caused the tea to go "swimming with the fishes" in Boston Harbor. It was just business. The only thing missing was the great Italian food.

But enough reminiscing, it's time for a rant. Although the times have changed, the people haven't. And by people I mean "We the People." Samuel Adams, the anti-politician politician, convinced the colonists that England was screwing them royally. The colonists missed out on a better deal because they blindly accepted what they were told. They never questioned Adams' motives or bothered to check to see if what they were being told was indeed true. Sound familiar? It should because politicians have counted on this aspect of human nature since the beginning of political campaigning. We'll revisit this in a later chapter.

And now back to our discussion of checks and balances. Did you ever wonder how much gets done when the executive branch of the government and the Congress are the same political party? It's only happened ten times in the last seventy years; the longest period being most of the sixties when we were just too scared to switch parties. The answer to the question is a little tricky. The quick answer is that a lot gets done. But the not so quick answer is just the opposite. Let me explain. In the short term, without the balance of meaningful dissension by the other side, a lot of legislation gets passed. This legislation is usually signed into law by the president. But for the most part it's usually quantity over quality. Think of it as new software that's rushed to market and is full of glitches and security flaws. The laws will still function, but not up to their full potential. The consumers of these laws, namely the American voters and their families, will register their discontent by voting the other side in within the next 2-4 years. After that, a lot of the previous legislation will be drastically changed to the point where it is almost unrecognizable. It's usually quite some time before that same one party sweep occurs again.

So it appears that political parties achieve substantially better results at the local level where the electorate and the politicians interact more with each other than with their respective parties. The further away that politicians move from the people and the closer that they move to the parties, the less effective they become.

So why do voters keep reinforcing this two party system? My guess is because voters are basically lazy. We've become comfortable with the two party system. We know who the enemy is and adding more enemies with more points of view would just confuse the issues. It's a love/hate relationship. We love being part of a party but we hate the party system. We get excited about party primaries and caucuses but we don't really understand how they work. The same goes for the

Electoral College process. And so we stick with what we know. We find a candidate who shares one or more of our views and we stay with that candidate.

But while we might find solace in our ignorance of the political process, political parties also find solace in our ignorance. Politics today, is a multibillion dollar business. It should revolve around the needs of the country but it actually revolves around power and influence which is another way of saying money. We have created a political machine that is more about the machine than about the people it was created to serve. By way of social media and psychological profiling, the political machine has learned how to control us faster and better than we have learned to control it. If it was a computer, we would pull the plug. Maybe that's not such a bad idea.

CHAPTER 2 – BRANCHING OUT

Sometimes I wonder what has happened to this country. We started out with such noble intentions. The Founding Fathers came up with a system of government that was "incorruptible." The plan was to have three branches of government. Each branch needed the other two to survive. In this system of checks and balances, the Congress would propose the laws and the President of the United States had the power to veto any perspective law that was seen as an overstepping of boundaries. Congress had the power to override that veto but it wasn't easy. An impartial Supreme Court had the obligation to nullify or let stand any law that was deemed to be unfair by "We the People." It was felt that the Supreme Court of the United States couldn't be subverted, until it was.

It happened slowly, over a long period of time. The political party siblings became more set in their ways as they grew up. Instead of growing closer, they grew further and further apart. They fought constantly and at times, hated each other. But they always loved their baby brother SCOTUS because he was always the voice of reason and never took sides. SCOTUS would always ask why circumstances and the situations surrounding those circumstances existed. He would don an impartial blindfold and weigh the validity of both sides on the ever present scales of justice. He did this because he loved both of his brothers equally, until the day that he started favoring one over the other. He shifted back and forth like a metronome while courting favors from both brothers. He did this so often that over time, he lost his own identity and ceased being the voice of reason that had defined him in his youth.

Nothing is black and white. Politicians and ratings hungry media like to make it that way because it is in their best interest for issues to be that way. It's also in our best interest. People like easy answers to complex questions but unfortunately, there are none. I've never understood this quirk of adult human nature. As young children, we ask why all the time. As we grow older, we stop asking and start accepting. The only people who still ask why are pollsters and, at times, reporters. Just about everyone else prefers to pledge allegiance to a party and be led by party leaders. Have you ever wonder why party extremes are called the radical left and the radical right? It's because people become radicalized by individuals who are masters of political manipulation for their own means. Perhaps you've heard of them, they're called politicians.

I began studying political science and world affairs in college. I've been studying those subjects ever since. I've learned that political rhetoric on either side, is nothing more than a smokescreen for politicians to cloud the issues and get elected. When I study a national or world event, the first thing I do is totally ignore the political rhetoric. I watch and read the news from both sides and no sides. And then it all comes down to the inevitable choice of the lesser of two evils. I don't mean that to be derogatory. I only used that expression to highlight the fact that there is no such thing as the perfect candidate or issue. Every political decision, no matter how big or small, will always be the lesser of two evils.

Politicians and political issues evolve over time. In the same way that I could never have written this book in one draft, it is unrealistic to believe that a politician will be totally defined on the first day that he or she takes office. By the same token, legislation isn't perfect the moment the ink dries. For example, Medicare was a disaster when it first became law. It was confusing and rife for abuse. It still is, more than fifty years later. But along the way, millions of senior and disabled Americans have lived healthier lives because Medicare came into being. It is a work in progress as is Obamacare, for tens of millions of previously uninsured or uninsurable Americans. Both plans have detractors who point out the many flaws, including increased costs to other Americans. But those detractors fail to realize that both health plans are works in progress that will never end.

If we were a country of robots this "imperfect" legislation would never be a problem, but we're not. As the diversification and needs of

Americans change, so does the legislation put in place to protect us. Unfortunately, the legislation doesn't always keep pace with our needs. Which brings up the problem of three branches of government that refuse to coexist for the betterment of the country.

Experts are quick to give a lot of reasons as to why our government has stopped working. They will tell you that politicians inside the beltway that surrounds Washington, DC, have lost touch with Americans who live outside of the beltway. They will tell you that the Republican Party, currently in control of Congress, has been hijacked by right-wing conservatives. They will tell you that the president of the United States has become frustrated with an unresponsive Congress and has taken to writing his legacy through the use of executive orders. All three of these reasons are partially true. But there is a fourth reason that is totally true.

Ever hear the phrase "politics makes strange bedfellows"? Have you ever wondered what that really means? Basically, it means that politicians will work with anyone, even people they dislike, if they find it advantageous to do so. And what is the number one reason politicians find it advantageous to work with anyone? The correct answer is money. Show of hands, how many of you got that right? Good for you! Now we'll take a short break while you run to the sink and wash the blood off your hands (yes, I am blatantly pandering to friends of Shakespeare). You see, dear readers, you're the reason they take that money. What's that? You've never forced them to take that money? The constituents doth protest too much, methinks (still pandering). When you look at the way that the political system works, you did.

Running for office is really expensive. It takes tens to hundreds of millions of dollars and contrary to popular belief, most political candidates don't have that kind of money. The ones that do, don't want to spend it on a 50/50 chance of winning. Even Donald Trump, who made a big deal out of saying that he could self-fund his campaign, is taking money from contributors (I wonder if he suddenly realized that a better investment might be to spend his money on the gaming tables at his old hotel). So it's no surprise that political candidates turn to the voters and, more importantly, special interest groups for the bulk of their campaign contributions.

Now a candidate can't generate enough cash by only taking ours. But there are plenty of people who have much more money than we do and by people, I mean corporations. In 2010, the Supreme Court of the United States (the baby brother, SCOTUS) ruled on Citizens United v. Federal Election Commission. At its core, attorneys for Citizens United argued that a nonprofit corporation should be considered a person for the purpose of campaign donations.

Basically, they wanted all campaign donation limits lifted for nonprofit corporations. Over time, that nonprofit distinction was broadened to include any corporations, organizations, labor unions, associations, secret clubs in treehouses, and the United Federation of Planets (notice how I snuck in a Trekkie pander). This allowed an entirely new generation of wealthy "people" to give an unlimited amount of money to political campaigns.

Now it's time for political candidates to go a courtin'. They dress up in their Sunday best and set out to find their perfect matches. But how do they know when they've made a love connection? That's where the voters come in because when it comes to setting up political candidates with corporate donors, we are all matchmakers. Without us, they would have no idea of what they want in a mate. The good news is that we have an extensive computer database of wealthy, single "people" who are more than ready to commit to a long-term relationship with Mr. or Ms. Right Political Candidate.

That old saying that there's someone for everybody is especially true when it comes to dating political corporate donors. It doesn't matter whether you're interested in healthcare or hand guns, saving endangered species or money on your fuel bill, cleaner air or air travel. And here's the best part about dating political corporate donors; they already know that you're only after them for their money! So what do they get from you? I'm glad you asked me that my friends. You know how you've always been told that you can't buy respect, you have to earn it? Well that's not exactly true in the world of political donor dating. In this world, money does buy respect from the people who take your money. So what does this respect do for a donor other than to boost their corporate donor ego? It also has the potential to boost their cooperate donor bottom line. It's as if all political candidates have read Dale Carnegie's book "How to Win Friends and Influence People" and they just can't wait to practice what they've learned on your behalf.

Now I don't want you to think that there's something underhanded going on here. Most of the time, there isn't. There are times when politicians will get caught up in the moment and go beyond the boundaries of a politician/donor relationship but those moments are few and far between. When they do happen, both parties find themselves in bitter divorce proceedings culminating in huge financial losses and/or career reversals. In extreme cases, they may find themselves with unforeseen roommates. But most of the time it's a symbiotic relationship that can help to forge agreements and deals which are beneficial to that politician's constituents. A problem arises when a politician's constituents become much more important than the country as a whole.

And for any politician, constituents are the people who make sure that they keep getting a paycheck. During congressional and senatorial election seasons, politicians are more worried about constituents in their home states than they are about the people of the United States. I once heard that party leaders start grooming politicians for the next election cycle on the day after they are sworn into office. I can't swear that it's true, but it wouldn't shock me if it was.

British Lord Acton once wrote, in a letter to an archbishop of the Church of England, "Power tends to corrupt and absolute power corrupts absolutely. Great men are almost always bad men, even when they exercise influence and not authority: still more when you superadd the tendency or the certainty of corruption by authority. There is no worse heresy than that the office sanctifies the holder of it." Lord Acton was referring to the actions of the church; but he could just as well have been referring to politicians who allow their actions to be defined by the office that they hold, rather than an obligation to the people that they serve.

But voters don't seem to care. We only care about how we personally benefit and the rest of the country be damned! We only care about whether it means jobs, an influx of money into our communities, or justification of a religious or personal prejudice. In actuality, we're more like pimps than matchmakers. We set up our politicians with lobbyists who pledge money to get what they want.

Every new session of Congress brings with it approximately 20,000 registered lobbyists attempting to sway politicians to their way of thinking. By the way, the term "lobbyist" is a throwback to a time when influence peddlers actually hung out in hotel lobbies and waited for politicians (now that really does make me feel like a pimp). Anyway, we take our cut in the form of less restrictive gun laws (NRA), more assistance for seniors (AARP), improved cell phone communications (Verizon) and much, much more. How much influence is gained is directly proportional to the size of the industry these lobbyists represent.

Now to be fair, not all of these attempts at gaining influence are bad for the American voter. Some service organizations do try to influence politicians to increase benefits and working conditions for their members. But conversely, some corporations are only looking to increase their bottom lines. The only certainty is that by the end of each session, someone will get a happy ending. And isn't that really what it's all about? Because we're not just talking about a few dinners or a private jet to a golf weekend. We're talking about loads of money to buy campaign ads and pay for campaign staff so that a few years down the line, politicians will still be able to buy campaign ads and pay for campaign staff. Get the picture? It's all about job security or more precisely, job insecurity.

And while we're on the subject of money, let's talk about the political action committee (PAC) and Super PAC. By the way, if you haven't already noticed, the one thing that politics and the military have one thing in common is that there are acronyms for everything. A political action committee raises money for a political race or issue. Now there are rules about who can donate, how much they can donate, how the money can be used, and what happens when then the race is over. In general, the rules are the same for a PAC and a SPAC. Neither PACs can have any contact with a candidate or the staff; but there is one glaring difference. You know the old saying that you can't take it with you? That doesn't pertain to a Super PAC. Super PAC money doesn't have to be returned to anyone. Any leftover funds can be used for just about anything. As far as I know, this loophole has yet to be abused. I have no doubt that this will change if given enough time. But since SPAC was spawned by Citizens United, my solution would be to get rid of Citizens United altogether.

In my opinion, there's just too much organized money being infused into and ultimately contributing to election results. We need to get rid of special interests and get back to the interests of the country as a whole. Political candidates rarely address this because doing so would jeopardize their ability to get elected or reelected by their constituencies. Which brings us back to our strange bedfellows saying. Apparently, politicians will sleep around for the right price. Try that outside of the beltway and you'll get arrested. But try it inside of the beltway and it will get you rewarded by the voters.

CHAPTER 3 – STOP THE PRESSES!

The off primary season is a lot like off Broadway except whereas off Broadway actors usually get a lot better, off primary politicians usually get a lot worse. The actors and politicians are similar in that they're all trying to make it to the big stage. The difference is that, assuming they put on a good show, most of the actors will make it. By contrast, most of the politicians will not.

And so our hearty band of politicians set out to cover the country (or the Midwest, whichever comes first) with their "give the people what they want to hear" rhetoric. And you can feel the love because at this stage of the game, it's as if you're performing for friends and family. It really doesn't matter how bad you are because your minions are still going to tell you that you're great.

It won't always stay this way because as the campaign progresses, the audiences can no longer be filtered for the purposes of media hype or ego boost. Future whistle stops will get progressively less friendly. It always amazes me that politicians aren't better debaters. Watching town hall meetings is like watching someone bounce a rubber ball off of a brick wall. Someone stands up and voices a legitimate complaint. What they're looking for is something other than what they can read off the Internet. They're not looking for talking points or party rhetoric. They want a real human being to give a really human response to what is, all too often, an extremely emotional concern. A good political debater could change an emotional concern into an intelligent discussion. But when candidates only stick to political rhetoric and prearranged talking points, they create an atmosphere of frustration and distrust.

The candidates act like they're actually concerned about the questioners' real problems. They're really not, but this is off Broadway and it's the best opportunity that candidates have to prove that they're just like the voters. When the caucus and primary curtain goes up, they'll go back to spouting party rhetoric and meaningless catch phrases. There will be more town hall meetings as the theater season moves on; but those will only be practice sessions to weed out the weaknesses of the paid political consultant dress rehearsals and ready the candidates for the nationally televised, political debate stage.

On the other hand, national political debates should be more like opening night. They're usually hosted by news organizations and moderated by seasoned reporters. They should be intelligent give and take between candidates but all too often, they end up being verbal cage matches. The answers resemble reconstituted rhetoric interspersed with insults. Keep in mind that debates only exist to convince undecided voters, those not affiliated with either party, to come over to our side.

The introduction of the candidates resembles the introduction of football players at the Super Bowl. The anticipation mounts as each player walks briskly onto the field of play. They line up while trying to remember all the plays that they learned during practice. It's all about keeping your eye on the ball. They glance nervously at the opposing candidates. The first play is fielded by the frontrunner. The possibility exists for a big gain but more than likely, the candidate will fumble and be tackled by the other candidates. Possession will change hands many times until, after about two hours, the game ends without any points being scored.

All kidding aside, these are well orchestrated media events. But outside of these staged events, the media plays a less visible but much more influential role in the outcome of political races. One thing I've learned in all my years as a writer is that no matter how objective you attempt to be while writing an article, the objectivity of that article will always be compromised by how much information you include and how much you leave out. For that reason, you can never achieve total objectivity.

When it comes to politics, the mainstream and alternative media platforms don't even try to be objective. On the Democratic side, Hillary Clinton gets more air time even though Bernie Sanders has more people at his rallies and wins more primaries. On the Republican side, Donald Trump gets higher ratings because of the outrageous things that come out of his mouth. With a couple of obvious exceptions, television is apolitical. The only numbers they care about are the ones that translate into higher ratings. Actually, that's not entirely true. Dig deep enough and you'll find networks that are owned by corporations that contribute hundreds of thousands of dollars to candidate campaigns. Sometimes they cover their bets on both sides. These candidates receive more air time. It may not seem like much but a minute here and a minute there adds up to a lot of minutes.

As for the other platforms, a lot of those Internet sites that may seem independent are actually owned by the same media conglomerates as the television networks. And if they're not, you really should pay attention to their advertising. It's an agenda influencing move that I call the Matryoshka Maneuver. Matryoshka dolls, also known as Russian nesting dolls, are a series of dolls that fit one inside of the other in ever decreasing size. That innocuous little ad that you hardly notice, may have ended up on that website through a progression of companies of ever increasing size. Which leads us back to corporations with an agenda. As the whistleblower Deep Throat once said to Bob

Woodward of the Washington Post, "Follow the money."

But there are times when journalistic integrity means little if a platform no longer exists on which to practice journalism. There's an old saying, "If a tree falls in the woods and a salaried reporter isn't around to report on it, no one will ever know that it fell." Okay, that's not really an old saying. I took poetic license in order to prove my next point.

The advent of digital online technology has left many print newspapers teetering on the brink of financial disaster. Even newspapers that have managed to establish an Internet presence have found it extremely difficult to develop a financially successful business model. With print subscriptions decreasing due to the more convenient and often free online news sources, more and more metropolitan newspapers have gone in search of financial bailouts. Sometimes, but not always, this can lead to a short circuit of journalistic integrity. In order to illustrate this, I'd like to tell you a story. It's a little something that I call "A Tale of Two Billionaires."

Once upon a time there were two billionaires. One billionaire was an industrious young man who made money selling products across a mythical land called Earth. Billionaire Bezos delivered his products far and wide through the sorcery of the

Internet and his magical sidekicks UPS, USPS, and FedEx.

The other billionaire was a distinguished, older gentleman who gave people a place to live (at least temporarily) in a mythical land called Las Vegas. Billionaire Adelson provided entertainment to the masses in the form of spinning pictures, dotted cubes, and small pieces of paper regaled with pictures of the royal family. His spellbinding games of chance could magically turn paupers into millionaires and back again.

Both billionaires sent town criers out to every corner of their kingdoms and the people rejoiced! That is until the town criers went on strike, demanding cost of living increases and a larger benefits package. The billionaires were baffled as to what they should do next. Seriously, they were baffled billionaires. They considered advertising for freelance town criers in local newspapers. And then, as if they were two billionaires with but a single thought, they decided that instead of advertising in the newspapers; they would buy the newspapers!

Billionaire Bezos bought the legendary Washington Post and declared, "I know nothing of this thing called journalism, but I do know of this thing called the Internet. Continue writing as you like and I will expand your words onto the Internet bigger and better than before!" And the workers rejoiced.

Billionaire Adelson bought the locally legendary Las Vegas Review-Journal and declared, "I know nothing of this thing called journalism, but it really doesn't matter. You have written unkindly of me in the past and I will make sure that this shall never happen again! From this moment on, you are prohibited from writing words against me." And the workers began to resign.

Hey, I never said that this story had a happy ending. I have no hard and fast evidence that this has occurred. But in a world in which perception can all too quickly become reality, the perception of what is happening at the Las Vegas Review-Journal is all too real. If this is indeed what Mr. Adelson had in mind when he purchased the newspaper, I would suggest that he look more closely at the example that Mr. Bezos has set for the Washington Post. Because if a newspaper loses its journalistic integrity, it also loses its credibility. If that happens, all he'll end up owning is a paper tiger instead of a newspaper.

I've related this fractured fairy tale in order to prove a political point. Sometimes you can't tell the political media players without a scorecard. A lot is known about the Washington Post. It was the home of Bob Woodward and Carl Bernstein during the Watergate era. I subscribe to the digital edition of this paper and I would have to say that the editorial content is somewhere to the left of center. I also live in Las Vegas, so I have more than a passing familiarity with the Las Vegas Review-Journal.

When I first moved to Vegas, I was hired to write a feature profile of casino owner Bob Stupak for the in-house Sunday magazine. Since that time, I have come to think of the RJ as a newspaper that is slightly right of center. There's also a slightly left of center newspaper named the Las Vegas Sun. Several years ago, both newspapers were brought under the same corporate financial umbrella but the editorial content remained separate. I believe that this is about to change. When Jeff Bezos bought the Washington Post, he didn't hide the fact that he was buying the newspaper. When Sheldon Adelson bought the Review-Journal, he used other people as go-betweens in order to cover his tracks. It took an investigation by RJ reporters before the truth was uncovered. Adelson is a conservative Republican with a very strong anti-Democrat bias. It bothers me when people with a political agenda attempt to hide the fact that they are buying media companies. I have begun calling the Review-Journal the Adelson-Journal. I fear that it's only a matter of time before it actually morphs into my sarcastic name for this newspaper.

It's not a question as to whether or not media can influence a political race because there is no question that it can. There's a reason why candidates spend hundreds of millions of dollars on political advertising. They're not going after the party faithful. They're going after the all-important undecided. Think about the decision process that you go through when you go shopping. If you're shopping for a television, that process usually starts with an advertisement. The next step probably involves reading product and customer reviews from a variety of online sources. Finally, it all comes down to a price comparison before your decision is made.

Much the same process is done when choosing a political candidate. I'd like to believe that the undecided voters look at most of the political commercials, debates, town hall meetings, and speeches. After which they probably talk to friends, read news stories, and watch media analysis of the candidates. Finally, after researching party platforms, they compare the two candidates and make a selection. I'd like to believe that without an allegiance to a particular party or issue, the undecided view elections with a little bit more clarity than their partisan brethren.

I'd like to believe this but I don't think that I can. In all probability, the undecided walk up to the voting booth with about the same degree of indecision that they've always had about the race. I think that the chosen candidate comes down to nothing more than a last second gut feeling. There is probably a quick mental checklist before sealing the deal. There might even be a last minute mental coin toss.

I believe that the undecided, much like the decided, don't believe many of the promises of any candidate. I also think that most voters think that they're nothing more than a small cog in a very big political machine; and that, ultimately, the machine will mold the winning candidate into its own image. In the end, I believe that 99.99% of the electorate decides a local, state, or federal election by choosing whichever candidate has mastered the art of media manipulation.

The question of whether or not the media contributes to the manipulation of the political system is not the real question. The real question is whether billionaires like Sheldon Adelson or Jeff Bezos are contributing to a political system that manipulates the media by influencing editorial content. Although not political in nature, Adelson has already exercised editorial control over the Review-Journal. Bezos has, as far as I know, not exercised any editorial control over the Washington Post. As print and other media platforms struggle to find financial life preservers, it will be interesting to see how media takeovers affect future political races.

CHAPTER 4 - THE AMAZING RACE

We find ourselves in the midst of another election cycle. It really doesn't matter when you read this, because we're always in the midst of another election cycle. Sometimes it seems as if election cycles have become so long that they practically connect with one another. The British have an election cycle that lasts about five weeks. Our average election cycle lasts anywhere from eighteen months to two years. This allows anyone who craves fifteen minutes of fame and has somehow managed to avoid getting their own reality television show, to put on a pair of Air America sneakers (yes, I just pandered to the CIA and Michael Jordan) and run a political foot race.

One of the fundamental tenets of being a human being is that we enjoy being noticed by other human beings. There's nothing wrong with that. Actually, it's a very good thing to be noticed by other people. It helps build self-esteem and, under optimum conditions, it helps an average person to evolve into a better than average person. That whole concept seems to go sideways when that same person decides to run for political office.

The rules that we live by on a day-to-day basis don't apply to someone running for political office. Most of us spend our days interacting with people who are familiar to us. When you run for political office, you find yourself interacting with political advisers, media coaches, and public opinion experts. Then you're expected to take all that you've learned and become someone who is everything to everyone. Think about it. Most people understand behavioral guidelines within a work environment. But politics is a bizarre environment where one wrong word, gesture, or awkward moment can turn your political dream into a political nightmare that will haunt you for the rest of your life.

At the beginning of the 2016 presidential race, a lot of people decided to run with the full knowledge that they couldn't possibly win. The Republicans had seventeen candidates at the beginning of this race. Imagine if you had seventeen children all vying for your attention. The ones that would get the most attention would be the ones who acted up the most.

Getting attention wasn't a problem for a publicity hound like Donald Trump (the only candidate who has actually had a reality TV show). He's spent his entire life figuring out ways to bring attention to himself. For the rest of the Republican candidates, breaking out from the pack was not an easy task. For one thing, Trump had a head start before he even got into the race. He knew the media and the media certainly knew him. They were counting on him to provide the comic relief in an otherwise boring political exercise. After all, how many times can you talk about Clinton and Bush and still make it seem fresh? The rest of the names, on both sides of the aisle, made a mortician convention seem exciting.

Deciding to get into a political race is a lot like that dream where you stand up to give a speech and suddenly realize that you're naked. You're going to end up metaphorically naked under a media microscope and even minor imperfections will end up in full view of the voters. Voters may overlook their own imperfections, but they'll never overlook yours. As a result, many good people who should run for political office will never even entertain the thought. So we end up with many of the same actors playing the same roles over and over again. But we should remember that the reason that they are there is because we put them in a position to be there. There is always a segment of American voters responsible for electing mayors, governors, and state senators. As much as we may yell about professional politicians, we are the ones who elect and reelect them into political office.

As of the last census, in 2010, there were approximately 309 million people in this country. About 219 million of those people were eligible to vote and/or run for some political office at the local, state, or federal level. In total, those three levels of government account for approximately 520,000 political offices. Now I'm no math genius, but that works out to about 24% of all the people who are eligible to run for office. Let's be generous and raise it to 25% in order to take into account all the people who run and lose. That means that a little more than 164,000,000 people, or 53% of our entire population, will never run for any public office. Think about that. More than half of our country will never run for even the lowest political office.

Okay, so maybe a job in politics isn't for everyone. I actually threw all these numbers at you in order to make a very simple point. As of 2010, 31% of voters identify themselves as Democrats, 29% as Republicans, and 38% as independents. This means that roughly 2/3 of all eligible voters disagree with the politics of any officeholder. Would you take a job if you knew that two-thirds of your coworkers didn't want you there? If you were really good at politicking, you might be able to convince half of the independents to agree with your way of thinking. Now, only one in two people wouldn't like you. I think I'd stay home in that case and that's exactly what most people do.

And so, for the most part, we end up with experienced politicians throwing their names into the political ring. Let's take a look at what the list of candidates looked like in the 2008 presidential election. John McCain and Barack Obama were U.S. senators. Bob Barr and Cynthia Mckinney were former U.S. Representatives. Chuck Baldwin was a pastor and member of the media. Ralph Nader was a consumer advocate and lobbyist. Four of the six candidates had experience with running and winning federal election campaigns.

In 2012, we had Obama running for reelection. We also had four former governors, two sitting governors, a former U.S. senator, two sitting U.S. representatives, one former U.S. representative, and a businessman.

This year, the field got really big. There were 23 candidates from the two major parties. There were seven former governors, five sitting governors, two former U.S. senators, four sitting U.S. senators, two business people, and a former neurosurgeon.

In all three races, the nonelected candidates were the least qualified people to become president of the United States. Even Ralph Nader, the lobbyist who had run for president on four previous occasions, had very few of the political skills necessary to run the country. Just as a doctor needs to go through a general medical school before choosing a specific area of medical care, the POTUS needs to know a lot more than how to run a business. In fact, that's probably the least important skill that a president needs to know.

The plain truth is that the voters are the least qualified people to choose a president. We have no idea what it's like to run the country. On average, less than 20 people will become president during a voter's lifespan. Are we really willing to risk an unqualified candidate being responsible for up to eight years of our lives? The risk can become multi-generational when a lack of world geopolitical knowledge leads to a war or economic downturn.

The Democratic Party seems to be coalescing around their presumptive nominee. Clinton's rival, Bernie Sanders, plans to become a driving force in the shaping the platform of the Democratic Party. But on the other side of the aisle, things are a little bit more complicated. Apparently, no one really likes their presumptive nominee. Donald J. Trump. But since he's all they've got, they have to do something to show some sort of party unity. One by one, the party leaders are selling their souls to the devil (that's only an expression, but you can take it any way you like). Every time Trump opens up his mouth and says something racist, they cringe a little.

You see, the race isn't only about the presidency of the United States. I think the GOP realizes that there won't be a presidential job opening for at least four years. The party leaders have found themselves caught between their public political careers and party politics. They don't agree with everything that their presumptive nominee says, but they have to support him in order to put up a front that the party is one. They also have to think about their own political futures. Which is why every time that Trump says something racist, they hurry to disavow themselves from his statement. The problem is that, as much as they may not like what he says, he is actually towing the party line. It's like the beginning of a Mission Impossible movie, when the Secretary sends Ethan Hunt out on a mission but disavows any knowledge of his actions if he gets caught. I have to give Trump credit for saying what the party is thinking, but it's kind of like a drunk uncle who blurts out all of the family secrets at Thanksgiving dinner. Some things should be left unsaid.

So we have a Republican Party that, although it looks united on the outside, is actually fighting a reenactment of the Civil War behind closed doors. It is a Republican Party that will have to begin thinking about a Reconstruction Era the day after the election. I think they should let the party crumble. In fact, I think that both parties should crumble. In the beginning, the two party system was a great idea. That great idea worked until the end of the twentieth century. I don't think it works well anymore.

Here's my idea of what would work better. Keep in mind that this will never come to pass. I'm just proposing a different way of doing things. Feel free to disagree or propose your own suggestions. So here goes nothing.

I propose that we get rid of the two party system. That means no more donkeys, elephants, or any other animal. Everyone should have an equal opportunity to run for political office. Despite what you may think, this doesn't exist in our electoral system. The opportunity to run for any political office should be open to anyone, whether they are homeless or a live on a palatial estate. But there is one thing that keeps this from happening and I will get to that in a moment. My election process would be overseen by the Federal Election Commission. Every potential candidate must pass a standardized test on their basic knowledge of how our government operates and global politics in general. Believe it or not, many candidates don't possess this basic knowledge. The potential candidates would only be allowed to take the test once. The window for taking the test would be from June 1 - November 30 of the year preceding the election. The ten highest scoring candidates would be allowed to run for any federal political office in the upcoming election. If candidates did not pass the test, they would not be allowed to run for any federal political office for a period of one year. The election cycle would run from January 1st of the next year until one week before Election Day.

Now let's talk about the one thing that keeps the average American from running for political office. That one thing is money and I have a radical proposal for correcting this situation. Keep in mind that I'm talking about candidates running for U.S. senator, U.S. representative, or POTUS. I propose that we get rid of Citizens United and every other method of fund raising. Now you're probably asking yourself how anyone could possibly run for office without any money. The answer is simple. If you're running for federal office, your campaign should be financed by the federal government.

Here's how my proposal would work. Upon passing the standardized candidate test, the top ten candidates would be given one million dollars which would come out of the federal treasury. This would be the only financing allowed for a political campaign. Any candidate who knowingly accepted campaign funds from any outside source would have to bow out of the race, return any remaining funds, and would be disqualified from running for office for a period of one year. Federal campaign money would be deposited into a campaign account in the same way that college students have scholarships deposited into student accounts. Every expenditure would have to be approved by the FEC and would be published on the FEC website. Proper money management would ensure that candidates would be able to finish the campaign process. It would also show the voters how well each candidate can handle a budget. If any candidate should drop out of the race, the remaining funds would be forfeited back to the federal government. Any funds remaining at the end of the campaign process would also be forfeited back to the federal government. This would level the financial playing field and allow anyone, whether they be unemployed or a billionaire, to run for political office. Media would be required to charge the same rate for every candidate and those rates would be capped by the FEC. Without political parties, the need for primaries, caucuses, and party conventions would no longer exist.

Now for the fun part. Voting would be done via the Internet and would begin one week prior to Election Day. The website would be overseen by the Federal Election Commission. Computers would analyze the social security database in order to determine who is eligible to vote. Voters would have twelve months prior to the election to verify social security number and address information. If the information on file with the FEC did not match the information entered at the time of casting the actual vote, that vote would not count. There would be no electoral college because the winner of the election would be determined by the actual number of votes cast for candidates. It would truly be a system of one person, one vote.

As it stands right now, our presidential contest is between a millionaire and a billionaire. Neither one represents the average voter. One is a former secretary of state with an expertise in geopolitics. The other claims to be an expert in business economics. The reason I say claims is because that candidate comes from the private business sector and information to back up this claim is not publicly available. Assuming that his claim is true, that expertise would be of some value to the country. But neither candidate can claim any degree of understanding of the other's expertise.

At the time of this writing, the voter favorability rating of both candidates is around fifty percent. For those voters who believe that every career politician is evil, this election will be the ultimate showdown between a political insider and a political outsider. One thing's for sure, it's going to be a bumpy ride for whomever is left standing on November 9, 2016.

CHAPTER 5 - FULL COURT PRESSED

The GOP in the final stages of the POTUS selection process. The party is in disarray and the candidates are sniping at each other like five-year-olds on a school playground. Republicans are trying to get back to their core values as a party, but extremists within the party are derailing every effort. Political debates are beginning to look like Jerry Springer shouting matches. The only saving grace in this whole process is that the party's rank and file is reveling in this departure from an otherwise boring election process.

Then the worst thing that could possibly happen to them actually happens. A leading advocate of the GOP's intertwined political and religious beliefs, ups and dies on them. To make matters worse, he happens to be on the Supreme Court of the United States. I mean he had the job for life! As a party, they hoped that the life part would last beyond the current presidential election cycle. But alas, such is life.

To be fair, I could have just as easily chosen a justice affiliated with the other side of the aisle because the degree of political influence is interchangeable; but fortunately (or unfortunately, depending on your political point of view) none of them have died recently. So let's take a closer look at the Supreme Court justice in question.

His name was Antonin Gregory Scalia. He was the only child of an Ellis Island immigrant father and a first generation Italian American mother. He was a good student who went from a Jesuit military school to graduating valedictorian and summa cum laude from Georgetown University. In 1986, then President Ronald Reagan nominated the former general counsel to former President Richard Nixon to the U.S. Supreme Court. He was deeply religious and extremely conservative in his political thinking.

As a Supreme Court justice, he was a strict constitutionalist. To put it simply, that means he believed that the Founding Fathers, who ratified the Constitution, had the uncanny ability to write a document that would never become societally outdated. Actually, it has more to do with how the Constitution is interpreted, rather than how it's written. To a strict constitutionalist, you can add amendments in order to address societal changes, but you can't interpret the Constitution in any way that would accommodate societal changes.

Let me choose a constitutional amendment as an example. Everyone knows the Second Amendment to the Constitution, "A well regulated Militia, being necessary to the security of a free State, the right of the people to keep and bear Arms, shall not be infringed." This amendment is actually made up of two parts. The first part is "A well-regulated Militia, being necessary to the security of a free State...." This was written before we had a standing army. We were basically a bunch of reservists who grabbed a gun when there was a threat to life, liberty, and the pursuit of happiness. Eventually, we built a standing army and no longer needed a well-regulated militia. The second part of the amendment is "…the right of the people to keep and bear Arms, shall not be infringed." The idea was that if there was any threat to life, liberty, and the pursuit of happiness; the men folk would be able to grab their guns and immediately form a well-regulated militia.

Strict constitutionalists believe that you should never interpret the constitution in a way that would remove any right that has been given to you by the Constitution. As with most things, that's open to interpretation. My interpretation of the Second Amendment is that you have the right to own a gun if you're part of a well-regulated militia. But a strict constitutionalist focuses more on the second part of the amendment stating that a person has a right to own a gun.

When this came before SCOTUS, of which Justice Scalia was a part, the justices ruled that the Constitution gave every American the right to own a gun. It was a majority ruling of a Republican controlled Supreme Court. Here's where I have a problem with any political control of SCOTUS. The Supreme Court of the United States is supposed to be an impartial legal body, but that rarely seems to be the case. We have more guns than people in this country. We have the highest rate of firearms related deaths and injuries in the world. And yet, a Republican controlled Supreme Court opted for political dogma over impartiality. I'm not saying that a Supreme Court controlled by Democrats would have been any more impartial. I'm pretty sure that it would have been just as partial to a liberal point of view. What I am saying is that a society that has moved from muskets to assault rifles needs to be more flexible in its judicial decisions, whichever political party is in charge. We are already seeing instances where society fails to keep up with technology. The Constitution of the United States will continue to be challenged. We need to ensure that when these challenges cause our Supreme Court justices do what's right for the country and not what's right for their respective political parties. But let's get back to reality and the current Supreme Court dilemma; what to do when a justice dies.

So now the GOP has lost a leading political advocate and a powerful opponent of a great deal of liberal legislation. And as if that's not enough, the POTUS that they've been fighting with for the last seven years has the power to nominate a more liberal thinking justice and change the entire political balance of the Supreme Court.

There's plenty of time to nominate a new Supreme Court justice. Normally, that wouldn't be a problem. But this isn't a normal time in political history. From a Republican point of view, with a little bit of luck, they could take back the White House. If that happens, there would be a Republican controlled Congress and White House for a couple of years. But that would be enough time to ensure a Republican nominee and a GOP majority in the Supreme Court for the foreseeable future. And if Republicans are really lucky, the next opening would be from the other side. Hey, I'm not being morbid; Supreme Court justices don't have to die because they can retire at any time.

Of course there is always the possibility that the Democrats will hold on to the White House. In that case, a liberal Supreme Court justice will be appointed and the balance of power will shift. This shifting of political power isn't what the Founding Fathers envisioned for SCOTUS. When the country was coming together, no one even considered that any of the three branches of government could corrupt the Constitution. They were building a framework that would enable the new American society to function. They thought that they had addressed all the problems that might arise and for the times that they lived in, they had.

But they never could have foreseen how the power of the people would transform into the power of the party. And therein lies the problem with the Supreme Court of the United States. The justices no longer leave their political and religious beliefs at the entrance to the most hallowed judicial chamber in the country. Let's take look at a sample of recent Supreme Court decisions.

Employee Paid Contraceptives: The Supreme Court ruled in favor of Hobby Lobby. This case focused on whether a Christian owned and operated company should be forced to pay for contraceptives for its employees, if those employees are insured under the Affordable Care Act. The corporation claimed that the ACA provision infringed on their religious liberty. This was a win for the pro-life, religious right-wing of the Republican Party. In case you're wondering if this is a direct violation of the concept of separation of church and state that is mentioned in the Constitution of the United States, it isn't. The Constitution makes no mention of a separation of church and state. The Constitution only forbids the government from sponsoring a religion or compelling an American citizen to join a religion. The vote was 5-4 in favor of the Republican majority.

The Confederate Flag and Freedom of Speech: This case focused on whether Texas could reject specialty license plates bearing the Confederate battle flag. The court ruled, in a 5-4 decision, that Texas could the reject those license plates. It's interesting to note that the four Democrats on the court were joined by Republican Clarence Thomas, an African-American. It's obvious that, when faced with a conflict between his personal and political beliefs, Thomas chose the former.

Race and Redistricting: This case focused on whether the Republican controlled Alabama State Legislature had redistricted high concentrations of black voters in some of its voting districts. The justices ruled that it had engaged in "racial gerrymandering." The vote was 5-4 in favor of the Democrats. The four Democrats were joined by Justice Kennedy.

Housing Discrimination: A Texas group claimed that their low-income housing vouchers were being rejected by landlords in white suburban areas because they were not required to accept the vouchers unless they accepted Federal tax credits. This case focused on whether a disproportionate number of federal low-income tax credits were being disseminated to landlords in minority neighborhoods. In a 5-4 decision, the court ruled that this was happening. The four Democrats were joined by Justice Kennedy.

Pollution Limits: This case focused on whether or not the Environmental Protection Agency had violated the clean air act. The court ruled that the EPA had failed to do a cost benefit analysis before setting stricter limits on pollutants from power plants. The vote was 5-4 in favor of Republicans.

Same-Sex Marriage: The court ruled that same-sex couples can enjoy the same right to marry as heterosexual couples, anywhere in the United States. The vote was 5-4 in favor of the Democrats. The four Democrats were joined by Justice Kennedy

There is an interesting aside to several of these Supreme Court decisions. I noticed that Justice Anthony Kennedy broke ranks with his fellow Republican justices on more than one occasion. Those occasions resulted in 5-4 votes in favor of the other side. I decided to take a more in-depth look at his background and found something that may help to explain this phenomenon.

Kennedy was nominated by President Ronald Reagan on November 30, 1987. Kennedy was confirmed by the Senate on February 3, 1988. At that time of his confirmation, there was a Republican president and a U.S. Senate controlled by Democrats. The confirmation vote was 97-0. One more thing, the confirmation of Justice Kennedy came nine months before a presidential election. I'm willing to bet that this moment in time, when politicians chose to do what was best for the country, has become indelibly etched in Justice Kennedy's memory. I guess there are times when Lady Justice really is politically blind.

Although the justices are evenly matched at the moment, that won't last for long. At this point, I should tell you that I don't have a PhD in American history or constitutional law. What I'm about to say is only an opinion and I welcome any comments to the contrary. In my opinion, the Founding Fathers created a deeply flawed judicial branch. Here's my idea of what would have worked better.

I think that the current but temporary configuration of the Supreme Court works much better. We have an equal number of liberal and conservative justices. You see, the Founding Fathers failed to realize that it's impossible to completely turn off a human being's belief system. Our beliefs, whether political or religious, become hardwired over time. Even if we had robot Supreme Court justices with artificial intelligence, it would be impossible to ensure that they wouldn't "learn" our human belief system if given enough time. The Founding Fathers believed that in the event of a deadlock, a ninth justice was the best solution. I believe that a better solution would have been to embrace party politics and require four members of each party be appointed to the Supreme Court.

So how would we overcome a judicial stalemate? My vision of SCOTUS would create a "ninth justice" comprised of the electorate. Once or twice a year, depending on the judicial workload, the voters would decide the outcome of any judicial decisions that were hopelessly deadlocked. There would be no campaigning or political party persuasion. The eight Supreme Court justices would submit two opposing conclusions for each case, directly to the

American voters. In order to ensure fairness, each conclusion would be submitted to the opposing quartet of judges for analysis and editing until both sides agreed on the wording. The wording of the conclusions would be written in plain English and absent of any legalese. In the unlikely event that voting ended in a tie, the case in question would be referred down to the district court for adjudication. The decision of that court would be final.

In fact, let's have some fun by trying my system out on an actual Supreme Court ruling. Recently, the eight remaining Supreme Court justices ruled on a case brought by the Obama Administration. In November of 2014, President Obama issued an executive order that gave temporary legal status and an indefinite reprieve from deportation, to millions of illegal immigrants. It applied to undocumented parents of U.S. citizens and permanent residents who had lived here for at least five years. It also allowed immigrants, who arrived as children and are under 30, to apply for a deportation deferral if they are living here legally. There's more, but that was the core of the argument. If my system actually came into being, there would be much more information.

Congressional Republicans claimed that Obama didn't have the authority to delay the deportation of this many immigrants without legislation. A lower court blocked the executive order. The administration appealed to the Supreme Court.

SCOTUS split straight down party lines; the four Democrats disagreed with the lower court, while the four Republicans affirmed the court's ruling. The deadlock allowed the lower court's ruling to stand. If you were the "ninth justice," how would you rule? Let me hear from you. The prologue of this book lists several ways to reach me.

So would my "ninth justice" idea ensure that the Supreme Court of the United States better represented the will of the people? Here's something to think about before you answer. A majority of voters, whatever their politics, believe that politicians become detached from the people who elect them to political office. They aim their frustrations at the executive and congressional branches of government. The judicial branch of government is largely overlooked because, for the most part, the justices operate behind closed doors and with very little fanfare.

In all honesty, it would be almost impossible to apply the same voting system to the other two branches of government. For one thing, the unilateral powers of the president are limited and, in most cases, only temporary. Whether or not you believe that a large percentage of congressional output is political posturing; the fact remains that the sheer workload of elected officials and their staffs would make a system such as I've described, completely unworkable.

But the Supreme Court is the only branch of government in which the electorate has absolutely no say in the matter. Wouldn't it be nice if we could change that? The ramifications of Supreme Court decisions can last over many decades and generations before they are ever challenged. Unlike laws that are designed to deal primarily with punishment, Supreme Court decisions deal with cultural and social changes. These decisions may not be as obvious to the average American citizen as are laws that deal with everyday actions.

Supreme Court decisions affect Americans on a far deeper level. These decisions permeate throughout our societal fabric and helped to create and expand an American sense of values to this country and the rest of the world. On the surface, a Supreme Court decision may appear to only deal with one individual or one company; but that decision will eventually affect many or all individuals and companies in this country.

CHAPTER 6 - WANTED: INEXPERIENCED PROFESSIONAL

Now we have a group of people yelling "Take back our country!" Funny, I've never been able to figure out from whom we are taking back the country. Let's be honest, we took the country. The only people who have a right to be yelling about taking it back are Native Americans. Considering that it was much less violent when they owned it, I don't think they want it back.

I've been wondering about this political catch phrase for, at least, the last twenty years. The best explanation that I've heard is that we need to take the country back from career politicians who are usually from the party that we don't agree with. But I really don't understand why being a career politician is a bad thing. Having a career means that you have learned your craft and have practiced it over a long period of time in order to gain experience. As far as I know, that's a good thing. People feel confident with doctors, lawyers, accountants, airline pilots, and just about every profession where the practitioner has had an opportunity to gain experience. Just about the only time that businesses prefer hiring less experienced employees is when they are instituting cost cutting measures or looking for an opportunity to either give on the job training or mold an inexperienced employee into the company image.

You would think that experience in politics is also good thing, but we have been conditioned to believe that it is not. We love to say, "Throw them all out." But no one would demand that every employee in a hospital be thrown out and new people brought in before a surgical procedure. You wouldn't want an inexperienced attorney if it meant the possibility of going to prison. You wouldn't want an inexperienced builder to build your next home. But we feel that way about our politicians; the men and women who, in one way or another, control just about every aspect of our daily lives.

So why do some voters want to throw out all the career (or as I like to call them, experienced) politicians? I mean let's be honest, voters put them there. The closest I can figure is that these voters are like children who, after not getting their way, look at politicians and say "I hate you!" Of course it may also be that some voters are impatient. It's easy to get behind someone who tells you, much like Aladdin's Genie, "Your wish is my command!" But there are no magic lamps in the real world; and solutions to problems don't usually happen in the blink of an eye. Then again, there could be a third reason that encompasses the first two and adds laziness to the mix.

"Idiots" and "morons" are the most common words that we use in referring to politicians we don't like. We say that they don't care about the country when they are politicians from the opposing party. We accuse politicians of manipulating us for political gain. All three of these statements are entirely correct. But all three statements are also completely misguided. For it is not the politicians who are guilty of these transgressions, it is the electorate.

The preamble to the United States Constitution reads,

"We the People of the United States, in Order to form a more perfect Union, establish Justice, insure domestic Tranquility, provide for the common defense, promote the general Welfare, and secure the Blessings of Liberty to ourselves and our Posterity, do ordain and establish this Constitution for the United States of America."

This was not written by accident. Words like we, union, general, and common were included to promote a sense of inclusiveness. The objective was to create a government of the people, by the people, and for the people. But our Founding Fathers always believed that the people would be well informed, open minded, and involved. Sadly, for the most part, we are not.

Most of us care more about being a member of a club, perpetuating opinions, and the excitement of jumping onto a candidate's bandwagon than we do about actual politics. We listen and memorize sound bites as if that's all we really need to know about any issue. We formulate uninformed opinions and then latch onto the nearest candidate who most closely matches those opinions.

Our political memories have a tendency to romanticize, sometimes even eulogize, the previous political party. And as with most memories, we have a tendency to forget the bad and remember only the good. In short, we yearn for change. That's one reason why the word "change" shows up in so much political rhetoric. It's the master political catch phrase of all time.

As I mentioned in a previous chapter, most of the electorate will never run for any political office; but that same electorate will take every opportunity to complain about those who do. While it may be okay for us to fail, it's never okay for a politician to fail. Which makes no sense because no one can live up to that standard. There are 535 politicians in the House of Representatives and 100 more politicians in the Senate. That's 635 politicians trying to make their individual constituencies happy. That is a recipe for disaster. Add to this that first year congressional representatives and senators are walking into a long established way of doing things but we still expect them to hit the ground running. As with any job, there is a learning curve and a seniority system. If a first term lawmaker wants to get anything accomplished, he or she has to convince a senior lawmaker to sign on. Unless the junior lawmaker has a foolproof way to obliterate the national debt before the next election, the prospect of partnering with a senior lawmaker is nothing more than a pipe dream.

The congressional mantra is "What's in it for me?" As selfish as that might sound, it is probably the only reason that anything gets accomplished in Washington. The real question that they're asking is "What's in it for my constituents that will make them reelect me?" Because when all is said and done, the only thing standing between a politician and the unemployment line is our vote. Each one of us has the power to impose term limits on a career politician. It doesn't matter how powerful or connected a politician appears. That politician is only one election away from rejoining the private sector.

Voter imposed term limits is something that requires minimal effort on our part. This is why I wonder why we complain so much about career politicians. We have the power to end their careers. And yet we like to complain that we are powerless when it comes to the political system. One of the things that the Founding Fathers did right was to ensure that we would always have that power.

I'm going to make a statement that will make at least half of the electorate shake their heads in disbelief. Are you ready? Again, half of the voters in the country will disagree with this statement. Every politician to ever hold a political office has done something good for a segment of American society, while occupying that office. In fact, I challenge any reader to name any politician, past or present, and I will give you a list of at least ten accomplishments that were good for some segment of the population. I'll go one step further. If I can't make good on my challenge, I will admit as much inside an autographed copy of this book.

Politicians really are public servants. They work for us all of the time. They just don't work for all of us all of the time. That would be an impossible task. Let's take a quick look at the latest U.S. census figures as of April 1, 2010. The makeup of this country was as follows:

Population 308,745,538

- Female persons 50.8%

- Persons under 18 years 24.0%

- Persons 65 years and over 13.0%

- White alone 72.4%

- Black or African American alone 12.6%

- American Indian and Alaska Native alone 0.9%

- Asian alone, percent 4.8%

- Native Hawaiian and Other Pacific Islander alone 0.2%

- Two or More Races 2.9%

- Hispanic or Latino 16.3%

Now imagine that you were the proprietor of an eating establishment. Let's call it the 'Something for Everyone Bar and Grill'. What would you serve? Let's assume that everything was made to order. How much time would you spend on each meal? Now, let's complicate things. If you could only afford the time and effort necessary to create one ethnic dish, which one would you choose? Let's go for broke. All these different groups come into your restaurant on the same night. Do you think that you could convince them all to eat the exact same meal? I'll make it easier. Could you convince a majority of your diners to eat the same meal? Probably not. But we have no problem asking our representatives in the House, Senate, and the White House to do just that.

Let's stay with our restaurant analogy for just a little longer. If some of your diners agreed to the meal of the day as long as you included a small side dish of their individual delicacy, would you do it? That's what is asked of our lawmakers for just about every piece of legislation. Every lawmaker has some piece of legislation that is important to the people back home. In case you haven't noticed, we are the people back home. We are the people who make passing legislation so difficult. We tell our lawmakers that we will gladly eat the main dish if he or she can arrange to get a side dish of our liking. In fact, we won't even ask the name of the meal du jour (yes, I've hit a new low; I just pandered to the French).

I leave it to the system of checks and balances to determine whether legislation and the riders (those little side dishes) attached to that legislation is in the interest of the country. With all its flaws, the system works most of the time. I don't even have a problem when the system doesn't work. There are times when a rider may have more impact than the legislation to which it is attached. The impact can be positive or negative. For example: a rider to lower automobile emissions standards could be attached to a bill authorizing more funds for cancer research. In this fictitious example, the long-term effects of increased automobile emissions would be more detrimental to Americans than would a short-term lack of research funding. We are left to rely on lawmakers to recognize and veto the implementation of this otherwise righteous piece of legislation. But is that really what they should do?

Our automobile emissions rider shined a spotlight on one of the complexities of our legislative process. You have to ask yourself who would stand to gain the most from lower automobile emissions standards? The answer isn't as cut and dry as it seems. The obvious answer is the automobile industry. Lower emissions standards would translate into lower research and car technology costs. These lower costs could be passed on to consumers in the form of cheaper automobiles. They could also be a source of greater profit for automobile manufacturers. If we take this a step further, cheaper automobile prices would lead to more sales of automobiles and higher stock prices. Higher stock prices would mean more dividends for private investors and 401K retirement portfolios. More dividends would lead to more consumer spending and a healthier economy.

On the other hand, more automobiles sales would lead to increased traffic on an already overtaxed highway infrastructure. This would lead to longer commutes, driver frustration, traffic accidents, and a possible increase in road rage incidents. In addition, studies have proven that increased car emissions are a contributor to global warming and health problems. This can lead to an increase in natural disasters thereby putting a further strain and increasing costs for first responders and our healthcare system. At this point, your head should be on the verge of exploding.

Taking all this into account, what would you do? Would you veto the cancer research bill or would you let it pass? These are the types of questions that the average American leaves to career politicians to decide. Of course, we can always clear the decks and elect a rookie Congress. Do you really believe that an on the job trained Congress would give us any more confidence in our lawmakers?

I guess what I'm getting at is that these "idiots" and "morons" may not always have the best judgment but then, neither do we. It's very easy to be a Monday morning quarterback and see what went wrong before saying what we would have done right. I don't always agree with political decisions. I probably disagree with a higher degree of Republican political decisions because of basic differences in ideology. But those differences should not manifest themselves in personal attacks and partisan gridlock. I may not always agree with all 635 members of Congress or the president of the United States, but I respect the job that they do. I couldn't do it and, judging by the number of people who run for political office, neither could the majority of Americans.

Are there some corrupt politicians? Sure. Is it time for some career politicians to think about retiring? You bet. But to blindly rid government of career politicians based on a belief that the alternative would be better, would be as ludicrous as only serving one meal to every patron in the 'Something for Everyone Bar and Grill'. With a little luck, you might be able to get away with it once before you would be forced to permanently close your doors.

CHAPTER 7 – THE UNITED STATES OF ANIMUS

I've always wondered why we pay so much attention to polls. They're like a guessing game where you only have to be correct 50% of the time in order to be considered an expert player. Sometimes you don't even have to be that good. Pollsters are like weather forecasters on local news. Even if you get it wrong, people continue to listen to you.

I always laugh when media outlets refer to their "scientific polls" because there's really no such animal. Let me give you an example of exactly what I mean. Here's a simple question, "What color is the sky?" You might think that the answer is blue. That would probably be the number one answer of most respondents. But answers can be based on everything from climate conditions to the location of the respondent to the time of day that the question was asked. Someone who has been in a windowless office all day might answer blue or undecided. There are always, at least, ten percent of the respondents who are undecided. You could ask "Are you breathing at this moment?" and at least ten percent of the respondents would be undecided.

Much like our sky color question, validity of polls can also be influenced by the political climate. Here's a little test. Ask ten people if Sirhan

Bishara Sirhan is a known terrorist. I'd be willing to bet that a majority of them will say yes based solely on his name. Truth be told, you could ask those same people if Sirhan is the president of Syria and a majority would say yes. It's not that the respondents are stupid; but they are influenced by mainstream media, social media and the opinions of family and friends. In point of fact, at least on the question of terrorism, they would be right.

Sirhan Sirhan was responsible for one of three high profile assassinations during the 1960s. Sirhan Sirhan assassinated Senator Robert F. Kennedy in 1968. James Earl Ray assassinated the reverend Martin Luther King, also in 1968. Lee Harvey Oswald assassinated John F. Kennedy in 1963. The heinous acts of these three gunmen terrorized the country for an entire decade.

The difference between then and now is that we didn't blame a religion or a country or an ideology for these senseless murders. We blamed the murderers. It didn't really matter if Sirhan was a Palestinian because we weren't looking for retribution. We were looking for redemption. The politics of fear and loathing didn't exist in American society back then.

Times have changed. I believe this is due, in part, to the mainstream media's rush to report the story before reporting the facts. We have created a 24/7 news cycle where the need for speed has become more important than a journalistic obligation to report the facts. When I was a journalism student at the University of Arizona, we were taught to gather all the facts before writing the story. Today's news outlets never let the facts get in the way of a good story. To that end, social media platforms have become an important ally in this revenue driven war of words.

When a news story breaks, platforms such as Facebook and Twitter allow a tsunami of opinion to rush into the factual vacuum. Any event involving American deaths immediately becomes a terrorist attack. The mainstream media uses the words terrorism or terrorist at every opportunity. They may use the word "purported" before the word terrorism but that's like hitting a Mexican piñata with a stick; children won't remember the hits but they'll remember the candy that fell to the ground. The media rushes to enlist a terrorism expert who is usually no further away than the nearest speed dial button. The expert will usually attempt to temper the interviewer's terrorism related questions with a sense of caution. But the interviewer will persist until that particular segment time limit is reached.

In essence, we have all become terrorism junkies. We no longer believe that a plane crash is just a plane crash. A despondent co-pilot flies into the side of a mountain and the mainstream media scours social media for any shred of evidence that the suicidal pilot had been radicalized by terrorists. A lone gunman kills 49 people in a gay nightclub and the media focuses on the 911 phone call in which he pledged allegiance to Islamic State. They completely ignore the fact that, in recent months, that same gunman had pledged allegiance to a half dozen other terrorism related organizations; some of which even fight each other. Hell, he would have pledged allegiance to the Nazi party if it was still in existence. Islamic State assumed responsibility for the attack. And why wouldn't they? This disturbed individual just pulled off the worst mass shooting in recent American history. That's what's known in the terrorism business as a freebie. In the 1960s, initial media reports would have called him a lone gunman. In 2016, that same lone gunman has been promoted to "supervillain."

Which brings up an interesting point (patience, I'm slowly leading you back into the subject of politics). Why is every lone gunman a product of the Middle East? The Middle East has given us the genesis of most of our scientific, mathematical, religious, and astronomical thought. But apparently, none of that matters. Now the Middle East is just the exporter of trained killers. I have a theory about this (but I'm sure you already guessed that). I'm going to get a lot of flak over this theory, but here goes. I believe that in the 21st century, Americans love to hate. After the events of 9/11, we went into a collective sense of shock. Politicians on both sides of the aisle exacerbated that sense of shock by lashing out instead of looking within. It's always easier to blame someone else rather than to blame ourselves.

We have been playing the board game Stratego (Google it) with countries in the Middle East for decades. In 1953, the CIA backed Shah Pahlavi in a coup d'état. Pahlavi appointed himself absolute monarch (that's never good). This led to an uprising, (okay, who didn't see that coming? Show of hands.), eventual exile, a 444-day hostage crisis inside the American embassy, and a resurgence of hatred towards the United States. (my, that went well). The only good thing to come out of the entire situation was the nightly news program 'Nightline with Ted Koppel'.

If you think that's the last time we screwed the pooch in the Middle East, think again. Iraq comes to mind along with Afghanistan, Libya, and Syria. They have all felt the heavy hand of Uncle Sam. The question is, why do we have a track record of messing up so badly in the Middle East? It's a rather simple answer. Getting down to basics, we just don't understand the political culture of the region because there is no political culture in the region. There are so many different religious warring factions that it's impossible to tell the players without a scorecard. Even if you do have a scorecard, it would probably be a lot easier deconstructing a spider's web into a single strand of spider silk.

The problem with our Middle Eastern political policy is that we tend to believe that the people of the region are just like us – they are not. That's not to say that, in general, they are better or worse than we are. All it says is that they do not share our political and cultural values. Here's a newsflash, they never will. But we always make the mistake of trying to impose a pseudo-democratic way of life as if it is a "magic bullet" for the region. And all we ever get for our efforts is more fighting and anti-American sentiment.

Franklin Delano Roosevelt once said, "The only thing we have to fear is fear itself." It was good advice then and it is especially good advice now. We have become a society that's scared of its own shadow, or rather the shadows of people we don't understand. But rather than trying to understand these people as individuals, we put them all in one group and identify them with one label. We do this because classifying people has been instilled in us almost from the moment that we were capable of cognitive thought. The labels that we learn include: boy, girl, pretty, ugly, thin, fat, smart, stupid, white, black, Jew, Catholic, Muslim, and the list goes on and on.

One day, an old friend told me that I was born Jewish. I told him that I wasn't born Jewish, I was born an Atheist. In fact, I continued, we are all born Atheists. He vehemently disagreed with my statement and questioned how I arrived at such a conclusion. I told him that newborn babies know nothing about religion. Most parents indoctrinate their children with the same belief system that they were indoctrinated with as children. He wouldn't even entertain the notion that I might be correct. I bring this up because I found an unsolicited book in my mail, today. An accompanying letter identified the author as an Israeli-American Jewish man. The form letter, which identified me as a "friend," went on to say "If you follow the advice of these ten Jewish people, I believe you will obtain the same results." Now I did not know this person nor had I ever requested his book. I am not a member of any Jewish organizations. To be totally honest, I identify myself as an Atheist. I can only assume that he subscribed to some database that identified my surname as Jewish.

I am also handicapped. I have never belonged to any handicapped organizations. The closest that I ever came was when my folks attempted to enroll me in a school that dealt with children affected with cerebral palsy. Notice that I said affected and not afflicted. Being afflicted with something puts you into a group. There isn't a person on this planet who hasn't been affected by something at one time or another. Anyway, the special school and I didn't last long. After about three months the school's director suggested that my folks think about other options. I won't go into detail, but my parents enrolled me in a public school kindergarten and I completed the rest of my education in public schools. I never regretted that decision because I grew up without the uncomfortable feeling that every minor accomplishment was worthy of a brass band and a presidential proclamation.

I was a handicapped immigrant in a non-handicapped land and I was encouraged to fit right in. Were there times when I needed help? Sure, plenty of them. And when those situations occurred, I readily accepted the help because I reciprocated the offer whenever I was asked for help. The question of race, religion, or sexual preference never entered my mind. I learned that when you need a helping hand, you don't ask too many questions. I didn't see a group. I only saw a person.

We have too many groups in the current political system. Maybe that's because there's safety in numbers and politicians feed on numbers. One racist is just a racist; but 1,000 racists are considered to be indicative of voter discontent and anger. That's nothing but a load of crap. They are just a large group of racists masquerading as concerned American voters. There are dozens of "concerned American voter" groups clogging up the political machine. These groups have personal not political agendas. But there are times when politicians from both political parties will use this groupthink for their own political gain.

The media and pollsters encourages groupthink, as well. They use fancy graphics and demographics to classify every American into some sort of a group. It's not enough to know how many Americans voted for a candidate or issue; we also need to know which groups voted for which candidate or issue. This parsing of data only allows it to be used as recruitment propaganda for more groupthink.

Now I understand that Americans become more afraid of terrorism after viewing news reports of domestic terrorist attacks by radicalized lone wolves. We should be afraid because these are frightening events. They are every bit as frightening as were the Columbine school shootings, the Aurora movie theater shootings, the Charleston church shootings, the Sandy Hook elementary school shootings, the Oklahoma City bombing, The San Ysidro McDonald's massacre; the list of senseless killings of Americans by Americans goes on and on. But we didn't rush to blame religious or ethnic groups as the perpetrators of those crimes. We blamed the individual criminals.

I believe that it is the media hype over these tragedies that exacerbates our fears. Unfortunately, tragedy also provides an economic boost across all media platforms. It's also unfortunate that tragedy unleashes the hypocrisy within all of us. It's an ugly side of human nature that we don't like to admit exists. We slow down to watch the aftermath of a traffic accident on the opposite side of the freeway. We're mesmerized by a tornado creating death and destruction in its path. And we're fascinated by every shred of information surrounding a mass shooting. If we weren't, the media information wouldn't exist because we are the economic boost that the media platforms crave. We pay for our indignation out of own pockets and then we choose to blame others for that indignation. It is the ultimate conflict of interest and it is hardwired into our DNA.

I believe that we watch these events with a sense of relief that it isn't us. It's a sense of (if you're religious) "There but for the grace of God, go I." It's also a form of survivor guilt coupled with helplessness. It is a moment of weakness that politicians are all too ready to exploit for political gain. They show us the path to inner peace by way of rhetoric and promises and we gladly follow. Alone, we may be fair and open minded; but groupthink has an insidious way of making us feel less helpless even if that feeling goes against our core belief system.

So we substitute animus for guilt and helplessness. Call me a cockeyed optimist but I don't believe that the majority of voters who lash out against religious groups and races, do so because they actually hold these beliefs. At least I hope not; if not for their sake, then for the sake of the United States of America.

CHAPTER 8 - POLITICAL CANDIDATES ARE GOOD KISSERS

Donald Trump is not alone in his ability to tell people what they want to hear. You don't have to be truthful when you're running for president. You can say anything you want.

Running for POTUS is no different from running for student council president while in high school. Your sole objective is to convince everybody that you are on their side. You do this by utilizing catch phrases that are easy to remember and as generic as possible. "A future we can believe in!" and "Make America great, again!" are two examples. Both catch phrases mean absolutely nothing. Change usually means of political party. Believing in something implies that you are constantly being lied to by the other party. Making something great again, usually means that the other political party did something to make America not so great. Since candidates of both parties tend to run on variations of these catch phrases at some point during their political careers, they are essentially saying that America has never been great because politicians from both sides of the aisle have always lied! About half the country swears by this this statement every four years. But let's stop and think about what this really means.

In an episode of the original Star Trek television series, Captain Kirk found himself and his crew being held captive by the ultimate computer (a blatant pander to Trekkies). This computer only knew the difference between logical and illogical statements. It was impossible to physically destroy the computer. So Kirk and the writers devised a more ingenious plan. Captain Kirk started out by telling the computer that everything he said was a lie. After a few seconds of pondering, the computer began questioning how that statement could be true if everything that Kirk said was a lie. Kirk kept pushing the fact that everything he said was a lie and the computer became trapped in an endless loop of trying to differentiate between what was the truth and what was a lie. Eventually, the computer imploded.

So what does this bit of imaginative science fiction have to do with a presidential campaign? Well if were to believe all the campaign rhetoric, then we would also have to believe that every candidate from either side of the aisle is constantly lying. There are plenty of people who do believe this. But this couldn't be true because we would, much like the computer on Star Trek, implode. Our economy and infrastructure would drop to zero and a Mad Max state of anarchy would prevail. This has never happened in our history. It didn't happen during the subprime mortgage banking crisis in 2007. It didn't even happen during the stock market crash in 1929.

Life was tough and rebounding was difficult. But we didn't implode because, despite all the political rhetoric that the parties put forth and the electorate loves to repeat, it became apparent that all politicians were not liars and our basic system of government worked. We began instituting new programs, new safeguards, and new laws. Slowly and deliberately we began to rebound. Within twenty years of the Great Depression, we became a world power and the mortgage crisis didn't diminish this standing.

So why do we believe all the campaign rhetoric? The answer is a very simple one. We believe all the half-truths because we want to. Period. We don't fact check our favorite candidates because we might not like what we find out. It's as simple as that. It doesn't really matter what side of the aisle you're on, what your religious beliefs happen to be, or whether the current fear of the month is real. All that matters is whether or not you believe your candidate. And we believe them because we want someone to think as we think. If we are a god fearing people, we want our candidate to be a god fearing person. If we are isolationists, we want our candidate to also believe in more restrictive borders and less job exportation. If we believe the government is too intrusive, we want our candidate to believe that government needs to be more hands off. In short, we want validation for the ways in which we think.

And so the candidates are all too happy to give us exactly what we want. According to PolitiFact, an independent and nonpartisan news organization, as of March 15, 2016, none of the presidential candidates come out smelling like a rose. Donald Trump's statements were true 2% of the time, Ted Cruz's statements were true 6% of the time, and the trailing candidate, John Kasich's statements were true 25% of the time. Don't think that the other side of the aisle came across much better. Hillary Clinton's statements were true 24% of the time and Bernie Sanders' statements were true 15% of the time.

So what does it tell us if the person who is least likely to become the Republican candidate for president is slightly more honest than the opposing party's frontrunner? More importantly, what does it say about us when we fall in behind candidates who choose to tell us the truth only about 25% of the time or less? I believe it tells us that, as voters, we don't care about truth. We care about what passes for truth. To quote a line from the first theatrical, full color movie that I ever saw as a child, Mary Poppins, the "spoonful of sugar that helps the medicine go down."

That movie was released about a year after the death of the Camelot White House and a week before a presidential election that would herald the beginning of the Vietnam anti-war era. The former was full of truths that we never knew existed and the latter was made up of lies that we wanted to believe existed. In the fifty years since, nothing much has changed. We still prefer to have our truths served to us with a spoonful of sugar or, as most often happens, served as lies dressed up to resemble the truth. In short, we want our political candidates to kiss up to us.

Which brings me to why I think political candidates are really good kissers. Let me explain. We all know the systems design mantra, "Keep It Simple, Stupid (KISS, for short). Well, political candidates have taken that to the extreme. Their mantra is, "Keep It Simple So Everyone Remains Stupid" (KISSERS). Political candidates are incredibly good at saying absolutely nothing while making it sound like they're saying something. For example, let's take a look at one of the issues that Bernie Sanders has put forth during this primary season. I'll get to the others in a minute, but this is a biggie.

"It's time to make college tuition free and debt free." This is where most of Sanders' youth vote is coming from. And why wouldn't they? The idea of not paying for your college education and seeing dollar signs afterwards is a very tempting proposition. Parents love it and so do students looking at the prospect of paying off a student loan over the next several decades. Racing into a career full throttle sounds great but let's take a closer look under the hood.

First of all, giveaways would only pertain to public institutions. You can't force private companies to give away their product for free unless you give them federal subsidies which, in the end, would be shouldered by U.S. taxpayers. While most universities do have scholarship programs, those are usually reserved for students who have good academic and/or athletic abilities.

A top athlete can bring tens of millions of dollars into a university by way of increased media exposure leading to increased visibility of all aspects of the university. This in turn, leads to increases in enrollment and research grants. Throw in licensing fees and donations from wealthy alumni fans and it's easy to see how a small initial loss can lead to long-term gain. College athletes who turn pro are forever linked with their university. From that time on, they become unpaid recruiters who will, by their very existence, lead to enrollment of more top athletes.

And remember those research grants? Scholarships for academic excellence can help cultivate gifted students into brilliant researchers in the fields of science and medicine. Scientific breakthroughs make worldwide headlines and lead to higher enrollment figures. Much in the same way that Las Vegas casinos will advance money to their high rollers knowing that they will probably get much more back in return, a top notch scholarship program will ensure that the house always wins. Without massive federal and state subsidies backed by taxpayers, public universities would struggle to achieve those same results.

Sanders also asserts that the free university system has succeeded in Germany. He is correct, but the reason is not as clear-cut as it seems. Germany is using the free university system as economic bait to catch American students. You see, Germany has an older population. They're looking for young blood and there's a lot of young blood in the U.S.A. that's looking for a free education. If American students go over to Germany in order to get their degrees, there's always a chance that they'll stay in Germany; at least for a few years in order to further their education or, best case scenario, practice their professions. That would give Germany enough time to recoup their investment and then some.

We, on the other hand, have a much younger population. Young professionals will eventually pay back a federal education investment by paying taxes and causing expendable income to make its way into the economy, but they would do that anyway. The flaw in Sanders' argument is that most American college graduates will remain in this country to practice their professions, whether their college educations were free or not.

And why do we have this mistaken idea that everyone should go to college? Let's use the automobile as an example. It's true that we need technicians, computer programmers, design specialists, and other college educated professionals in order to build tomorrow's automobiles. But we also need people to work on assembly lines (robots can't assemble every aspect of an automobile), sell the automobiles, and service the automobiles. While some technical training may be necessary, an all-encompassing college education is not (the same argument could be made for computer programming). These people also pay taxes and inject expendable income into the economy.

But there's another reason why a college education may not be for everyone. While having a degree may look good on a resume, it may not necessarily mean that it was the best training for your chosen career. Take my degree for example. I received a Bachelor of Arts degree in journalism from the University of Arizona. It was a very good education. I learned everything from the inverted pyramid (an exercise in taking a broad subject and, eventually, getting to the point) to journalism ethics. I thought that having a degree would validate me as a reporter and writer.

My very first professional article was returned to me with the word "sophomoric" written in red pencil across the top. I didn't even know what sophomoric meant. I was sure that it didn't mean anything too bad until the Merriam-Webster dictionary set me straight. The definition was, "Of, or relating to, a sophomore in college."

Seriously? I was way past that. I had a piece of paper that said I was way past that. And yet, there it was; I had failed my first test as a professional writer. Fortunately, the magazine editor gave me a shot at redemption. I could rewrite the article and resubmit it. In the spirit of desperate times call for desperate measures. I threw out all the rules that I'd learned in journalism school. In their place, I substituted the little "voice" that's buried deep within all writers. That voice was shaky and unsure of itself but the clock was running down and all I had left was a literary Hail Mary. That fly by the seat of my pants rewrite began a two-year stint as a columnist and feature writer. In fact, that same magazine approached me to write an article for their 25th anniversary issue!

Don't get me wrong. I loved my years at the University of Arizona. My eyes were opened up to a world view that I never knew existed. In fact, I switched from wanting to become a law researcher to wanting to become a journalist because of that view. But I question whether or not I could have achieved that outcome in ways other than a college education.

I grew up in a time when the pathway to a career ran straight through a university campus. I no longer believe that a college education is a prerequisite for a successful career. Don't get me wrong. There will always be a need for universities to provide an education for professionals such as doctors, lawyers, teachers, researchers, scientists, and a host of other careers. But I don't believe that federal money is best spent on subsidizing this level of education. I would prefer to see more federal subsidies go to apprentice training programs. My dad never went to college but he was smart and a fast learner. The army took those traits and turned him into an engineer. He used that skill to rebuild our home whenever a wheelchair or long-legged braces made it a necessity.

And I would like to see more money spent on all levels of education below the college level. Too many good teachers are burning out early. The ones that remain, find themselves trapped between high levels of bureaucracy and low school budgets. It's a sad statement on our society when underpaid teachers are expected to work long hours, under enormous pressures in order to mold young minds with inadequate or antiquated learning tools. They then find themselves using their own money to pay for school supplies. I would have more respect for Bernie Sanders if he proposed fixing education at its root rather than pandering to young voters in his base. And he is not alone in the practice of trading empty promises for votes. Every candidate in every race puts forth great sounding but impractical proposals meant solely to pander to a segment of the electorate. If you give the people what they want, they will never question if what they want is what they really need.

And there are times, as with Donald Trump and the Great Wall of Mexico, that it's necessary to convince the voters that they need something they never knew they wanted. Trump loves to talk about rapists and drug dealers coming across the border from Mexico but he fails to talk about the migrant workers in the fields of California. Those are the migrants who work long hours under extremely hot sun and for low pay. Those are the migrants who pick the food that ends up on our dining room tables. They do a job that most Americans would not do without cost of living increases and a benefits package. There are two sides to Trump's wall but he'll only show you one.

Even though I think that Sanders and Trump are on the wrong side of the issues, at least they take a stand. The list of Clinton issues is so safe that I fully expected a unicorn to jump off the page and go running around my office with rainbows shooting out of its ass! Who doesn't think we need to do something about Alzheimer's disease, campus sexual assault, affordable health care, and LGBT equality (although Obama pretty much got the ball rolling on the last two)? Mix in the universal fear factor of immigration reform and national security; add a generous dose of more support for veterans and disability rights and you've got a veritable smorgasbord of political comfort food for thought. She does talk about early childhood education but makes sure to mention that "every child deserves the chance to live up to his or her God-given potential." Are you listening religious right?

By now you're starting to get the picture of how all candidates are good KISSERS and avoid, to use a phrase from a former political candidate, "inconvenient truths." As the people ultimately responsible for these candidates getting into office, we could stand up and demand that they don't make us promises they can't keep and that they don't try to scare us with situations that don't exist. We could do that but we won't. Because, in the end, it's the promises that make us happy and the irrational fears of the present that make us believe that the future will be better.

CHAPTER 9 - THE FICKLE FINGER OF FATE

We believe that voting is a right in this country, it isn't, Voting is a privilege that, on average, 60% of us take for granted every four years. And in between those four year spans, even less people vote. They use the excuse that it's not going to change anything. Actually, we're just lazy. Most voters won't take the time to learn more than the one issue that they really care about. And even if they do take the time; it still depends on the weather, what sports event is on television, or just about anything else that's going on in their lives. But the excuse is always the same, it's not going to change anything. Wrong. People can't change anything if they don't vote.

We don't know much about the African continent in this country. Most of us don't know the names of the dozen or so countries where thousands of people die each year as a result of terrorism. What's more, we don't care. We also don't care how many people die in Mexico as a result of drug cartel related terrorism.

We don't care about these people because they don't share American values. Yet many Africans will brave the threat of death just to get an ink stained finger that symbolizes the fact that they went out of their way to vote. And many Mexican politicians will risk being gunned down by drug cartels when they attempt to fight the corruption that runs rampant throughout some Mexican states. It turns out that it's Americans who don't value our values.

In 2012, only 53.6% of the 84.3% of eligible Americans went to the polls. That same year in the Netherlands, 71% of the 74.6% of eligible Dutch citizens, turned out to vote. In fact, according to the Pew Research Center, the United States was ranked 31st in voter turnout on a list of 34 countries. Only Japan, Chile, and Switzerland had a lower voter turnout in 2012.

These non-voting Americans don't understand how a slight uptick in American voter turnout can affect our economy, our military capability, equality of races and gender, quality of our education, the safety of our infrastructure, and whether or not our cities can withstand a natural or man-made disaster. I know this because it's happened in the past.

In 1952, the population of the United States was 157.6 million people which is roughly half of what it is today. And yet, 18% more people voted in that year's presidential election than voted in the presidential election of 2012. Not that it mattered because nothing much happened during President Eisenhower's tenure. Here's a small sample of what I mean by nothing much:

- The Department of Health, Education, and Welfare is created

- The Refugee Relief Act of 1953 admitted 214,000 more immigrants than permitted under existing quotas (we survived that quite nicely)

- The Federal Aid Highway Act provides federal funding for construction of interstate highways

- Social Security begins for people over 65 and the disabled

- Congress sanctions the "Eisenhower Doctrine" in order to assist in protecting friendly governments in the Middle East

- The Civil Rights Act of 1957

- Alaska becomes the forty-ninth state

- Hawaii becomes the fiftieth state

But there's more to this story. All this, and more, was accomplished by a Republican president and a Republican Congress for the first two years; and a Democratic Congress for the next six years. In those days, politicians were more concerned about the country than they were about winning. Now I'm not saying that there weren't contentious moments, there were. But the disagreements were debated and negotiated until both parties and the president were satisfied with the outcome. They did their jobs without personal animus or stonewalling.

Eisenhower was an incredibly popular Republican president who was elected to office in an overwhelming landside. Under the circumstances, one could probably assume that it would have been very easy for him to push Republican agenda legislation through a Republican controlled Congress and vice versa; but Eisenhower admitted that during the first two years of his administration, his harshest critics came from within his own party.

That doesn't happen today. We live in an era of political partisanship above all else. Blatant stonewalling has taken the place of political discourse. Shutting down the government is used as a political weapon in order for political parties to get what they want. Political parties use the American people as metaphorical hostages in order to negotiate partisan deals.

Despite all that's wrong with our political system, it pales by comparison to other countries where political parties actually do hold their citizens hostage for political gain. There are countries where political party members can be in power one day and in jail the next. Actually, those are the lucky ones. In many countries, the political opposition will never make it to jail.

But the fickle finger of fate doesn't only apply to countries where the threat of imprisonment or death hangs in the balance. In those cases, you pretty much know where you stand. One side makes the rules and the opposition decides whether to adhere to those rules or defy them. The penalties are well known to both parties. In most cases, the toppling of a leader takes military might. The rules aren't always that clear in a democracy. Case in point -- Brexit.

Brexit, a catchy word for British exit, was an idea that probably sounded a lot better on paper. It came about as a result of Prime Minister David Cameron's attempt to quiet the United Kingdom Independent Party during the 2015 election. He promised to hold a referendum (issue advisory vote) on whether or not the United Kingdom should remain in the European Union. It was a bold gamble that would ultimately cost him his political career.

But what exactly is the European Union? The forerunner of the current day EU was formed in 1957 when the Treaty of Rome was signed between Belgium, France, the Federal Republic of Germany (West Germany), Italy, Luxembourg, and the Netherlands. The European Community was established in 1967. At the time, it was felt that the best way to avoid a World War III would be for many of the European countries involved in the previous World War to band together into a unifying economic and mutually beneficial trade community. Sir Winston Churchill envisioned it as the framework for a "United States of Europe." In 1973, Britain joined the European Community. In the years that followed, free movement of goods, services, citizens, and capital was initiated between these countries. All this led to the formation of the European Union in 1993.

Great Britain remained in the EU for the next 23 years. And then, along came Brexit. The IN or OUT referendum focused on fear over facts. The IN campaign focused on economic collapse; while the OUT campaign focused on the country being overrun by Middle Eastern immigrants. The truth is, no one really knew what would happen if the UK left the EU. Fear will always fill a factual vacuum. Each side countered the other's doomsday facts with their own non-doomsday facts. It would have been comical it wasn't so serious. Before we laugh at how naïve the Brits were, we should take a long and hard look into our own political mirror.

In 2004, President George W Bush ran a reelection campaign based on one simple concept, the terrorists win if we change leadership. The worst terrorist attack in United States history had happened less than three years earlier. The economy didn't play a major role in that year's election because the terrorist attack had been a major disruption to the economy. The subsequent war in Iraq was a valid military action because we were going to get the people who did this while, at the same time, stripping Saddam Hussein of any weapons of mass destruction that could be used against us in a future attack. After the reelection of President Bush, we learned that none of the attackers had come from Iraq and we had no evidence that Saddam Hussein still had WMDs. But patriotic fervor and the fear of change had worked.

Politicians use one of two tactics when running for office -- promise or fear. We've already seen an example of fear so let's look at an example of promise. One that comes readily to mind is, "A chicken in every pot and a car in every garage." That was part of a 1928 campaign ad "promise" during the presidential campaign of Herbert Hoover. It was a thinly veiled promise of economic prosperity for everyone. Hoover won a landslide political victory.

Let's play a little game. We've seen how promise or fear can fuel a presidential victory. And we've seen how increased voter participation can elect a candidate and an opposition Congress with only the interests of the country at heart. Now I'm going to describe a candidate who campaigned on promises and tapped into people's fears. This candidate not only won the election, he also brought unparalleled prosperity to the voters. Let's see if you can tell me the name of this person.

Our candidate ran during a period of economic downturn. After winning the election, he came through on his promises. Groundbreaking social and economic programs were instituted. The mass transit infrastructure was expanded. He increased employment by instituting government backed construction projects. His administration put limits on the number of hours that employers could require employees to work. It also gave employees more benefits than they ever had before. He stripped undocumented aliens of rights reserved for citizens and prevented them from taking jobs away from those citizens. Industrialists, such as Henry Ford, supported his administration in newspapers and financial contributions. The economy flourished and he was hailed as a man of the people. Okay, what was the name of this politician?

I'll give you a few hints. We've already discussed how the Eisenhower administration gave us the federal highway system and Social Security. The Franklin Delano Roosevelt administration gave us the Works Progress Administration (later renamed the Work Projects Administration), employing 8.5 million people over the eight years of its existence. The WPA was responsible for the construction of everything from highways to libraries, the Griffith Observatory in Los Angeles to playgrounds and school lunch projects, the Lincoln tunnel in New York to the Federal Writers' Project (yes, I am blatantly pandering to my fellow writers) and much, much more. FDR also gave us the Public Works Administration responsible for, among other things, building the Boulder Dam (later renamed Hoover Dam) in Boulder City, Nevada (I had to put in a blatant pander to Boulder City. I live right next door in Las Vegas). By the way, it wasn't either of these politicians.

I will give you one final hint.

First they came for the Socialists, and I did not speak out—

Because I was not a Socialist.

Then they came for the Trade Unionists, and I did not speak out—

Because I was not a Trade Unionist.

Then they came for the Jews, and I did not speak out—

Because I was not a Jew.

Then they came for me—and there was no one left to speak for me.

Friedrich Gustav Emil Martin Niemöller

Martin Niemöller was a theologian who initially supported our mystery politician. He later regretted that decision and turned against the NAZI party. If you haven't figured it out by now, the politician who came to power by way of promises and fear was Adolf Hitler.

As Americans, we view past hybrid regime leaders (elected leaders who became authoritarians) such as Hitler, Hugo Chavez in Venezuela, Otto Pérez Molina in Guatemala, as moments in history. But there are 36 hybrid regimes in the world today. These regimes are located in Central and South America, Africa, Eastern Europe, even the Pacific Island of Fiji is a hybrid regime. The leaders of these countries enter into office by way of Democratic or pseudo-Democratic elections. While they may keep some of their promises, they have a tendency to reap more of the benefits of those promises than do the people who put them into office.

Promises are the lifeblood of politics. In most cases, it is the only thing that will separate one candidate from any other candidate. Unfortunately, most of these promises will never have the remotest chance of ever becoming a reality. Promises get their power from hope, need, or misguided beliefs. Free college tuition is a promise that sounds great to many young people who have little or no income. But totally free colleges will never become a reality. It would be an economic nightmare for taxpayers and it flies in the face of free enterprise, the core of a capitalist system. And yet, tens of thousands of college students banded together in support of a candidate who made such a promise. These were not stupid people but they were hopeful and needy people. The Great Wall of Mexico is another promise that will never see the light of day. It would also be an economic disaster that would end in failure. I say this because no wall, no matter how tall or how wide, will ever keep out desperate people with nothing to lose. But many Americans continue to believe that Mexican immigrants take away American jobs. This despite the fact that studies show that most Americans don't want to bus tables in restaurants, make beds in hotel rooms, or pick fruits and vegetables in orchards and fields for twelve hours a day.

As for Brexit, the die has been cast. The UK still has a way out because this wasn't a binding vote; it was only an advisory referendum. A new referendum would probably go the other way. They can still turn back before Cameron or a new prime minister invokes Article 50 of the EU Treaty. Then there is no turning back. But this probably won't happen because too many political dominoes are beginning to fall. Brexit may become another example of "Be careful what you wish for, you may just get it."

The ironic thing is that the people who were most responsible for allowing the referendum to pass, are the people who will, most likely, benefit the least by its passing. Sixty-one percent of the people who voted to leave the European Union, were over 65. Most of them were blue collar, less educated, and retired or poorer than their counterparts. Seventy percent of the people who voted to stay in, were young, college educated, and moderately successful in their careers. New economic trade and service agreements could take 10 to 20 years to complete. The majority of Brexit voters have already reaped a lifetime of benefits from membership in the European Union. In return, they gave an extended middle finger to the people most likely to have to live with the consequences of their action. How's that for a fickle finger of fate?

CHAPTER 10 - (or 11, you make the call)
THE TRUMP CARD

As I write this, Donald Trump is the presumptive GOP nominee for POTUS. As the primary season progressed, I watched news reports from around the world. When it came to Trump, they kept coming back to a central but perplexing question. They all asked how this man could keep coming up with one outlandish statement after another against religions, cultures, and individuals and still win primaries. I wondered this as well. And then it hit me -- Don Rickles.

For those who don't recognize the name, Don Rickles is an insult comic whose career has spanned six decades. During that time, he has successfully lampooned presidents, celebrities, and the average person. He has never been politically correct in his act. I'll give you an example of exactly what I mean. He once said of an audience member, who would be referred to today as obese, "… stick a cord in her navel, stamp Goodyear on her ass, and hope to God that she takes off." A statement like that would have been greeted with disdain if it had been said by anyone other than Don Rickles. But the audience had come expecting to hear this from Rickles. Indeed, they would have been disappointed had they not heard something like this come out of his mouth. Everyone laughed, including the woman.

People had paid to be a part of his audience. Some had even hoped that they would become part of his act. They were never disappointed.

Which brings me back to Donald Trump. Trump is a narcissistic. He craves publicity. Why else would a billionaire want to be a reality television star? Running for president of the United States is the ultimate high for a narcissist. The whole world is watching. When you're in a crowded field of potential candidates, the only way to stand out from the crowd is to be outrageous. Trump knows this from being a reality television star.

In my opinion, he never wanted to be POTUS. About a month before he became the Republican presumptive nominee, this was backed up by his ex-communications director in an open letter to Trump supporters. So why would he run for a job that he doesn't want? If you're Donald J. Trump, the answer to that question is a no brainer (take that any way you wish). There is a high level of visibility while running for president of the United States. You can be in front of a television camera on a daily basis. You can say things that aren't true and you can promise things that you can't deliver. You can do this because you are not performing any job that requires accountability, dedication, or adherence to any job standards.

Being president of the United States is another matter. You are a diplomat, a pragmatist, a world leader. The anything goes attitude of the primary season is over. Day-to-day activity is more solitary. Television cameras don't chronicle your every word. Your world becomes less about you and more about, well, the world.

Donald Trump has said that the political system is "stacked against me" and accused the Republican party of conspiring to stop him from clinching the party's nomination. At a CNN town hall meeting which included members of his family, Trump said "I know the rules very well, but I know it's stacked against me by the establishment." His daughter, Ivanka, criticized as "onerous" the New York registration laws that kept her and her brother Eric from casting primary votes for their father. Apparently, she got her beauty from her mother and her petulant attitude from her father. She learned to blame everyone else for her own failures. I am really surprised that Trump hasn't begun to blame others for his biggest failure yet; his inability to stop from becoming the Republican presidential nominee. He's tried hard but he has failed and now Trump is trapped.

Donald Trump has been trying to fail since day one. He tapped into the dormant volcano of a small group of American voters most of whom were as close minded as the man they support. He knew that, as the alternative candidate, he would get a lot of media and Internet attention. He planned on being the political gadfly, the anti-politician politician.

He wanted the publicity. All he's ever wanted is publicity. He already had it in New York. Then he got a network television show and his name recognition increased. But it wasn't enough. It's never enough if you're a narcissist. So he latched onto the Obama birth certificate conspiracy and watched his name recognition grow even larger. But again, it wasn't enough. He had to rely on the various media sources having the desire or time to promote him. He had no control over their editorial meetings and the birther crap was beginning to run thin.

What you have to understand is that Trump's need for publicity is equivalent to a teenage boy's craving for sex; it is always on his mind. And then it dawned on him. The media loves a presidential primary season, especially when the primary season begins about a year earlier than the actual primaries. It's reality television at its best (or worst) and really helps to fill a 24-hour news cycle. It was also national publicity that he could buy. And so he threw his hat into the ring and, much like that teenage boy, approached the presidential primaries with a very limited understanding of the process and no experience. He really didn't care. After all, he didn't plan to get that far into the process before he dropped out of the race. And then something happened that even he hadn't expected. The ugly American raised its ugly head and started a groundswell of support for him. I have to believe that this took him by surprise. But the media ate it up and Trump loved the fact that the media was feasting on him.

Now he had a real problem. What if this fun and games primary season potentially ends up in the White House? There would be no cameras in his face on a daily basis. Once the pomp and circumstance of inauguration day ended, he would be dealing with paperwork, meetings, and tough decisions. Even he could see that being POTUS happens mostly behind closed doors. The media is no longer there to chronicle your every word. He could pull a Richard Nixon and wire the White House but if he dropped his guard and inadvertently said something Trumpish, it probably wouldn't end well.

And then there is the actual work of being president. Trump has never done an honest day's work in his entire life. I realize that there are many ways to take that statement. I only meant it in one way. It's up to you to figure out my meaning. Anyway, there's a reason why presidents of the United States age relatively quickly while in office. It's a very stressful job. It's not as easy as saying "You're fired!" on a reality television show. There are no producers and directors making all the decisions. You are the producer and the director. The consequences of your decisions will affect millions of people long after those decisions are made.

But his supporters will argue that the successful businessman Donald Trump can make America great again. Wait, actually it's Trump who says he can accomplish this because he is a successful businessman who has made much more money than Forbes magazine says he has made. In order to find out if a successful businessman could accomplish great things, I did a little research of my own. I decided to see how his qualifications stacked up against another successful businessman, Bill Gates.

I started out by going to Google. I found numerous references to Bill Gates as a business leader, philanthropist, entrepreneur, investor, and computer programmer. Next, I did the same for Donald Trump. I found numerous references referring to him as a real estate developer, television personality, and author. Round one goes to Bill Gates

Then I looked at their educational backgrounds. Trump attended the New York Military Academy and went on to attend Fordham University before transferring to the Wharton School of Finance at the University of Pennsylvania. He graduated with a degree in economics. Bill Gates went from public schools to a college preparatory school to Harvard University. He dropped out of college and formed a partnership with another college dropout, Paul Allen. Trump wins round two.

Finally, I looked at their business backgrounds. Trump parlayed his economics degree into a job at his father's company. After inheriting $250 million, he followed in his father's footsteps and has become a successful real estate developer worth somewhere in the neighborhood of $10 - 40 billion (depending on whether you ask Forbes magazine or Trump). Bill Gates and his partner created a software program for a computer they couldn't afford to buy. They convinced the computer manufacturer to test the program. This led to the creation of a software company that eventually became Microsoft and made Bill Gates one of the richest men in the world. Moving on.

Both men have used some of their incredible wealth for the betterment of mankind. Bill Gates, along with his wife, started the Bill and Melinda Gates Foundation. The foundation assists in providing medication and scientific research to needy people around the world. Donald Trump occasionally gives children rides in his private helicopter. To be fair, not much is known about Trump's philanthropic endeavors because he refuses to release his tax returns. Rather than speculate, we'll just call this one a draw.

So let's compare the two businessmen in terms of their ability to keep their businesses running. Gates remained with Microsoft even after he was no longer president of the company. The company grew stronger and still exists. Donald Trump has declared bankruptcy on four businesses within the last twenty years. While this may be considered a normal practice in the world of business, the lessening or elimination of debt by payment default is not considered to be a good way to run a government.

You just can't run a government in the same way that a business is run. For one thing, you don't have the power to make all the decisions. Business owners have the latitude to hire, fire, or give work related incentives to employees. They can change suppliers or unilaterally make a decision to cut down on operating costs. The president of the United States does not have that kind of freedom. Donald Trump may believe that his business background is what's needed to, as he puts it, "make America great again" (the necessity of which is debatable, depending on your party affiliation); but those skills are a minuscule part of a POTUS's job requirement.

There is one criteria in which I was able to find common ground between the two billionaires. For all of their money, neither one of them seems to be able to get a decent haircut. Now I'm not saying that you need to get a $200 trim like Bill Clinton did (and we all know how much Clinton liked to get a little trim) or a $400 haircut like John Edwards (what is this Democratic fixation with hair?); but even a $15.00 Supercuts special would look a hell of a lot better than the bowl on the head thing that these guys seem to be doing.

Donald Trump touts himself as a political outsider. There's no such thing when you're running for president of the United States. I prefer to call him an anti-politician politician. As I mentioned earlier, I don't believe that not having political experience is a good thing. Being POTUS is the highest political job that we have in this country. You wouldn't want your neurosurgeon to just have a basic understanding of human anatomy. Then why is it okay for a presidential contender to just have a basic understanding of politics and government?

Even if we put Trump's many flaws aside for the moment, he doesn't have the most basic skills necessary for the job. I've been studying world and national politics for almost forty years but without any practical experience, I wouldn't even consider myself qualified for the job of president of the United States. I'm not trying to be clever (okay, maybe I'm trying to be a little clever), but this is not the best time in our history to be debuting a new reality TV show "Donald J. Trump, POTUS Apprentice."

I understand that a lot of Americans are upset by real or perceived problems within our federal government. As I said earlier, all politics is local. Many Americans are dealing with problems such as crime, drugs, and unemployment on a daily basis. But there are no quick fixes, especially from a man with absolutely no experience.

Many of Trump's supporters see him as the Lone Ranger ready to ride into Washington on his white stallion. But even the Lone Ranger was knowledgeable in and followed the rules of law, justice, and fair play. He was a fictional character who reflected the political and cultural mores of the time. From what I have seen, Trump seems to believe that those cultural and political mores don't apply to him. He believes that might makes right; that the same negotiating skills he uses to construct a building can be used to deconstruct a nuclear threat posed by a man who doesn't think twice about killing his own relatives if they get in his political way. If he really believes that Kim Jong-un will negotiate with him because he is Donald J. Trump, then he is either extremely naïve or the biggest narcissist to walk the face of the earth.

One of Trump's basic negotiating tactics is to "fight back very hard" if negotiations don't go smoothly. That might work well in the business world because buildings don't bleed. But in the geopolitical world of today, fighting back very hard will get innocent people killed. At the very least it will get us involved in a conflict that will cost us more treasure and blood than we can afford to lose. Do we really want a leader who believes it's acceptable to negotiate with people's lives as if they were buildings?

I believe that the political fervor over Trump will dissipate when the reality of what he represents finally sinks in. This may not happen until voters are actually standing in front of the ballot that decides the course of our country for the next four years. It's easy to get caught up in the poll and ratings driven madness of the primary season. It's a lot more difficult when the madness ends and the only thing left is a choice between rhetoric and responsibility for your future.

EPILOGUE

Here's how to have a political discussion with someone of an opposing political belief and still remain on friendly terms.

Them: "So what do you think of the election?"

You: "This is the craziest race I've seen since, well, ever."

Them: "I think Trump is (substitute Clinton for Trump) going to take it all."

You: "I don't think so. I mean, he's (she's) got a small group of strong supporters within the Republican Party (Democratic Party), but beyond that..."

Them: "I think the country will vote for him (her)."

You: "Eventually, he'll have to release his tax returns (she'll have to deal with the email investigation) and that might hurt him (her)."

Them: "No, he's (she's) got it."

You: "Who knows? This whole race is just too crazy."

Them: "You're right about that. Well, I've got to go."

You: "Have a nice day."

Them: "You too. Take it easy."

Notice that at no time was anything about politics actually mentioned. Nothing relating to the future of the country or its citizens was discussed. The entire conversation, which actually took place, focused on nothing more than whether or not the election was crazy. It remained friendly and non-confrontational because neither party said anything of any great consequence. Instead, the focus was on topics that would have absolutely nothing to do with either candidate's ability to run the country. This is all the American voter cares about. I should add that I am pretty sure that a variation of this conversation would also work when discussing religion but, since I have not tested this theory, use it at your own risk.

If you haven't already noticed, I've been pandering to different groups throughout this entire book. According to Wikipedia, "Pandering is the act of expressing one's views in accordance with the likes of a group to which one is attempting to appeal." I began with Star Wars fans and moved on to Trekkies, the disabled, Shakespeare enthusiasts etc. I made a point of mentioning it every time I pandered to anyone. I even put my most blatant panders in parentheses. You'd be correct in thinking that I was joking, but I was also trying to make a point.

As soon as I mentioned your group or interest, a little microburst went off in your brain. You felt good because for that nanosecond, I was just talking to you. That's exactly what political candidates do to you with catchy campaign slogans like "Make America Great Again!" and "Hillary for America!" It's as if we didn't know that Hillary was for America. Now I may not be the brightest bulb in the box but I figured that out when Hillary (who doesn't need a last name because we're obviously old friends) decided to run for POTUS. A little aside here, Ronald Reagan's campaign slogan was "Let's Make America Great Again!" Apparently, America has to be made great again immediately following a Democrat as president.

Getting back to pandering. I did one blatant pander throughout, pretty much, this entire book. You probably didn't notice because it was my most reoccurring pander. Can you guess what it was? I spent a lot of real estate in this book, pandering to someone who claims to know a lot about real estate. That's right, I blatantly pandered to Donald J. Trump. Basically, pandering is the act of giving someone what they want; Trump wanted publicity and so I gave it to him.

I'm not embarrassed by this admission. The media has been pandering to Trump since he first entered into the presidential race. So have his rivals from both sides of the aisle. More importantly, so have his supporters. We have all been pawns in the biggest publicity stunt of all time! Now before you dismiss this statement as nothing more than a mere guess; let me give you a little insight into how I arrived at this conclusion.

Donald Trump is not a stupid man. I know this because he reminds us of that fact at every opportunity. Aside from that, he did need some intelligence in order to become a global businessman. So why does he continue to insult and demean everyone outside of his Republican core support base? His false bravado and arrogance are not exactly endearing character traits. By his own admission, he is a master negotiator. Hell, he wrote a book about negotiating; he called it 'The Art of the Deal,' not 'How to Kill the Deal.' He wouldn't walk into a boardroom and immediately start insulting the other side. And yet that's exactly what he's done since the first day he entered the race. The only thing that made any sense was that he wanted to be in the race, but he didn't want to win.

And make no mistake about it, he has tried every trick in the book in an effort to lose. Short of shooting himself in the head (which would only seal the deal for gun rights voters), he has used every other tactic he can think of to lose. He's even fired his campaign manager with less than six months to go before the election. That's like firing your coach a month before going to the Super Bowl.

But what I couldn't figure out was why anyone would enter a race as important as this one, if they never intended to win. The answer dawned on me as I passed the golden façade of Trump tower near the Las Vegas Strip. It's not about the race, it's about the Trump brand.

Keep in mind that this is a man has spent a lifetime branding his own name. He puts it on everything including hotels, clothing, golf courses; the list goes on and on. He does it all with an unbridled glee that only a narcissist can have. There's only one thing that he's never been able to brand with his name; and that is the lips of every man and woman in the civilized world. And now he's managed to accomplish this feat. Some may cheer and others may cringe at what he says, but everyone is talking about him. I have to give credit where credit is due. Donald J. Trump, candidate for president of the United States, has pulled off the ultimate publicity stunt.

I predict that Donald J. Trump will suffer a resounding defeat this November. His "failure" to take up residence in the White House will happen because he wants to lose. Winning was never part of his game plan. His plan from the day that he first entered the race was world name recognition. The billionaire who boasted that he could self-fund his entire political campaign, has converted a $50 million campaign loan into a contribution. While $50 million may sound like a lot of money, it pales in comparison to what he will reap in return for being a worldwide media fixture for an entire year. It may turn out that he has a lot more in common with some of our Founding Fathers than I originally thought. He understands that sometimes, it's only business (without all the great Italian Food). This may be the first presidential race in American history, where only one party nominee ran as a serious candidate. But that fact won't stop many, many people from analyzing the entire race for decades to come. Because out of that analysis will come much better ways of manipulating a voter's psyche.

Because Trump's publicity stunt exposed the dirty little secret of running a political campaign in the twenty-first century; psychology is more important than political knowledge. Fortunately, at least for the moment, publicity stunts won't get you elected. This may change as voters become more and more complacent with these types of political races and campaign managers become more adept at running them.

Politicians have always used some degree of psychology in political races. They tell you what you want to hear. Rather, they tell you what they believe you to want to hear. And if by chance they say something you really don't want to hear, they will do one of two things. The first thing they'll do is say that they were either misquoted, taken out of context, or just plain misunderstood. If that doesn't work or if political party pressure becomes too great, they will either issue an apology to whatever group they offended or they will stay with their position but couch it with an "understanding" of the other side's point of view.

Even if reporters or social media platforms continue to remind voters of the original indiscretion, they will point to the follow-up mea culpa as proof of their contrition. If all else fails, they can always throw a political Hail Mary pass which is the act of showing a little humility and confessing to being only human. Voters eat this up because we have an unrealistic yearning to believe that politicians can relate to all of us. Most politicians don't relate to the average American at all but as long as we believe they do, we're good.

The point I'm getting at here is that you shouldn't let political candidates use your brain for their own political gain. Use your own brain. Research beyond what you believe. Go outside your own political box and take a peek inside someone else's. At the very least, you may learn that you like something about the other candidate. And if that doesn't happen, it will only serve to reinforce everything that you already believe. What do you have to lose?

Now I realize that there are people who won't vote because they don't care for either candidate. This is a really selfish thing to do. There are senior Republican Party members who have publicly stated but they will refrain from voting in this presidential election. They view this as a protest against a presidential candidate that they really don't support. They are being selfish in two ways, not voting and for publicly stating that they're not going to vote. By not voting, they are exhibiting a complete disregard for the people who fought and in some cases died so that we would have the right to vote in free and fair elections. Some voters may say that they want to "take back our country" from an unseen enemy that has taken America away from us; but even fighting non-existent enemies is a lot better than being a non-voter who has no problem turning his or her back on one of the basic rights that makes the United States of America, truly the land of the free.

Maybe this is just another milestone in, what I call, the dumbing down of America. The Vietnam War, the Democratic convention riots of 1968, the assassinations of the Kennedy brothers and Martin Luther King within a five-year time span, and the civil rights movement are nothing more than mere footnotes in a history book that most Millennials will never read.

As for the rest of us, well, American voters have very short memories. What memories we do have, usually has to do with one or two incidents that we either liked or disliked about a particular candidate. In this year's race, the issues are Hillary Clinton's personal email server and Donald Trump's connection with the possible improprieties of Trump University. While these issues may have some degree of importance in a general sense, neither of them has anything to do with whether or not either candidate can perform the job of president of the United States.

Let's look at some past issues that have been considered important by voters and the media. In 2012, the issues were whether President Barack Hussein Obama was born in the United States and former Governor Mitt Romney's personal parking garage. In 2008, the issues were whether President Obama was born in the United States and whether former Alaska Governor Sarah Palin, could actually see Russia from her front porch. In 2004, the issues were whether U.S. Senator Barack Obama was really born in the United States, whether President George W. Bush looked good in a flight suit, and whether Governor Howard Dean knew the proper way to yell (or, some would say, scream) when trying to motivate his base. In 2000, the issues were whether State Senator Barack Obama was actually born in the United States, Governor George W. Bush had phoned in his National Guard service, and whether Vice President Al Gore was going all "Henny Penny" about global warming (it turns out that he wasn't, but that's for another book). I can't make this stuff up, folks. These were actual non-issues that the media and voters talked about all the time (I may have exaggerated the length of time that anyone cared about President Obama's citizenship, but you get the picture).

This November, we'll either elect a man who will make America great again, again or a woman who is actually for America (as opposed to all the other male presidents who, unfortunately were not). What gets lost in all the regurgitated slogans and vapid rhetoric is that this is not an election for the United States of Trump or the United States of Clinton. It is an election for the United States of America.

The U.S. Constitution begins, "We the People of the United States, in Order to form a more perfect Union…." Everyone is familiar with the first seven words but in my mind, the next eight words are even more important. Those words, "in order to form a more perfect union," are a lot more powerful than they seem. The Founding Fathers could have said in order to form a perfect union, but they didn't. They viewed America as a work in progress that would never end.

The Founding Fathers didn't have a crystal ball. They could never have imagined the trials and tribulations that this new country would go through as it expanded across the continent. They couldn't imagine the depth and breadth of the threats that this new nation would face from outside and within its borders. They couldn't foresee our country being torn apart by war, prejudice, religion, and politics. But they also couldn't foresee an America that would weather it all and become a world power.

The Founding Fathers created a blueprint for a new society. They knew that this new society would go through growing pains as it matured. They also knew that this society, this union, would never be perfect. But they knew that, "We the People of the United States, in Order to form a more perfect Union, establish Justice, insure domestic Tranquility, provide for the common defence, promote the general Welfare, and secure the Blessings of Liberty to ourselves and our Posterity..." would never stop trying.

If I was running for POTUS, my completely unique campaign slogan would be, "America (blatantly pandering to Americans), we're still working on it!" I probably wouldn't get elected.

And with that, I will end my reminiscences and rants about politics. Actually, I think I feel a new rant coming on.

www.ingramcontent.com/pod-product-compliance
Lightning Source LLC
Chambersburg PA
CBHW071408280526
45787CB00001B/487